UPDATED EDITION

THE

UNITED STATES

OF

CRAFT
BEER

UPDATED EDITION

THE UNITED STATES OF CRAFT BEER

.....*A Guide to the Best*.....
CRAFT BREWERIES ACROSS AMERICA

Jess Lebow

ADAMS MEDIA
NEW YORK   LONDON   TORONTO   SYDNEY   NEW DELHI

Adams Media
An Imprint of Simon & Schuster, Inc.
57 Littlefield Street
Avon, Massachusetts 02322

This Adams Media trade paperback edition August 2020

ADAMS MEDIA and colophon are trademarks of Simon & Schuster.

For information about special discounts for bulk purchases, please contact Simon & Schuster Special Sales at 1-866-506-1949 or business@simonandschuster.com.

The Simon & Schuster Speakers Bureau can bring authors to your live event. For more information or to book an event contact the Simon & Schuster Speakers Bureau at 1-866-248-3049 or visit our website at www.simonspeakers.com.

Maps © 123RF/Rainer Lesniewski; Bigstock/Lesniewski
Brewery photographs supplied courtesy of the respective breweries

Manufactured in the United States of America

10 9 8 7 6 5 4 3 2 1

ISBN 978-1-5072-1529-6
ISBN 978-1-5072-1530-2 (ebook)

Beer consumption and industry statistics courtesy of the Beer Institute and the Brewers Association.

INTRODUCTION

Beer is truly an international beverage.

In ancient Egypt, beer was a form of sustenance, a bread-like liquid that could nourish the body and salve the soul. It was also a form of wealth. Workers were paid for their efforts with a daily ration of beer. Overseers, government functionaries, and elites were paid more than they could possibly drink, allowing them to in turn hire servants or trade their excess for other items of value.

In the 1400s in Germany, beer was such an important part of daily life that it sparked the creation of the oldest food law still in existence—the Reinheitsgebot. This ancient law, passed in 1487, lays out not only what can be put in beer but also set rules for the sale of beer and the cost of a liter of the stuff. Hundreds of years later, beer's importance to German culture had not diminished, and it was with this frothy beverage in 1810 that wedding-goers toasted the marriage of Crown Prince Ludwig to Princess Teresa—the very first Oktoberfest.

In the late 1800s and early 1900s in America, beer and its alcoholic brethren were considered the work of the devil, giving ammunition to the temperance movement that swept the nation and eventually led to one of the darkest periods in American history—Prohibition and the Great Depression. In the 1930s, when Prohibition was ended by the Twenty-First Amendment, taxes on the revived beer industry helped pull the country, and eventually the world, out of their collective economic hole.

At the time of the American Revolution, before the bottle cap and before there was a distribution infrastructure, there were literally thousands of breweries in America. People bought their beer at their local taverns because it was difficult to package and transport beer very far, thus creating the need for so many breweries. During that dark, dark time of Prohibition, the number of breweries in America dropped to single digits, all of which turned to producing other products in order to survive.

Today, things have vastly improved, and we finally have more breweries in the country than we had during the Revolutionary War.

In the past few decades, there has been a renaissance in beer brewing in the United States. New flavors, new styles, and new breweries are popping up every day. Collaborations are taking place—oftentimes between brewers on opposite sides of the nation or even on different continents. Prospective brewers can attend universities dedicated to teaching the arts of craft brewing, and record numbers of students are graduating from these programs.

Though beer is brewed all over the world, and the origins of this beverage are far from the shores of this country, it is my belief that in no other place can you find such innovation, such craftsmanship, and such a wealth of good beer as is now in America.

This wasn't always the case. In the 1990s, if you traveled to Europe and offered to buy someone in France, Germany, Italy, or Belgium an American beer, you probably would have been laughed at. But that's only because the beer aficionados in those countries were unaware of the growing wave of craft brewing that had picked up momentum. Most of the rest of the world knew only of the big, commercially produced American beers. But times have changed. Information moves fast, and so do cans and bottles of beer. Though your local bottle shop may not stock all of the beers from all of the breweries in this book, many of them have found dedicated followings far from home. It is now possible to enjoy cold, craft-brewed American beers as far away as Shanghai, China, or even the remote islands of the Maldives. And while the joy of craft beers sometimes comes down to the fact that the beer in your pint glass can only be found at your local brewpub, I find it comforting that the American beer renaissance has spanned the globe and has finally put to rest the question of whether or not Americans can make good beer.

—Jess Lebow

ALABAMA

Straight to Ale, Huntsville

⭐ ORIGIN

For the better part of the twentieth century, beer of 6% ABV or higher was illegal in the state of Alabama. Home brewing was also illegal in the state. In fact, it wasn't until the Gourmet Beer Bill was pushed through the state legislature in 2009 that breweries were allowed to raise the alcohol content of their beers up to a monstrous 13.9%. It took until May 2013 before Alabama finally became the forty-ninth state to legalize home brewing.

Of course, when the Eighteenth Amendment to the Constitution was enacted in 1920, marking the start of Prohibition—one of the darkest stretches in modern American history—home brewing, along with commercial brewing, was made illegal in every corner of the nation. When Prohibition was repealed by the Twenty-First Amendment thirteen years later, brewers focused on returning commercial production to pre-Prohibition levels—not only so that the thirsty masses could finally enjoy a bit of legal suds again, but also to help raise needed tax money that would eventually help lead the country and the rest of the world out of the Great Depression.

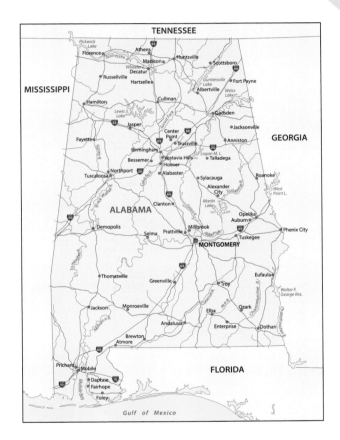

Perry filled out the paperwork and began the process of creating Straight to Ale.

WHY WE LOVE THEM

Straight to Ale is the brewing equivalent of the boy who never wants to grow up—the adult who remembers what it means to play hard and have fun, who makes up the rules to a backyard game of hide-and-seek as he goes along to add just another little pinch of magic into a classic we all love. The company's beers are inventive and fun. It's named for cofounder Dan Perry's childhood memories of monkeys and dogs who were shot into space and dreams of becoming an astronaut.

The brewers take risks and try experiments—like aging their Russian imperial stout and saison in barrels previously used for tequila, rum, bourbon, and wine. It's this kind of thing that keeps bringing me back to the beer store. It's this kind of creativity that turns an afternoon of sipping beer from a just-having-a-cold-beverage experience into exploring the recesses of the human taste buds. It's this kind of beer that draws us to craft brews in the first place—because they are different and dare to bring something new to the barbecue.

It might surprise you to know that it actually took another forty-five years (until 1978) before the laws governing home brewing began to catch up with those governing commercial breweries. And it took another forty-five years before Alabama home brewers would enjoy the same protections as the rest of the country.

What does all this have to do with Straight to Ale? Well, as you might expect, the founders of the brewery were themselves home brewers. They were active with brewing lobbyist groups like Free the Hops, groups that eventually managed to put enough pressure on the state's government to get them to enact the laws allowing higher-alcohol beer and home brewers to peacefully coexist in Alabama.

So it was in 2009, on the Monday after the Gourmet Beer Bill was passed, that Dan

Straight to Ale delivers three categories of beers:

- "Core," which includes Monkeynaut (IPA, 7.25% ABV, 75 IBU), Stout at the Devil (oatmeal stout, 7.8% ABV, 21.7 IBU), Chill Pils (pilsner, 4.5% ABV, 15 IBU), and Brother Joseph's (Belgian dubbel, 8.0% ABV, 24 IBU).
- "Seasonal," which includes Blood Brother (Belgian-style dubbel, October through December release, 8.0% ABV, 24 IBU), Regal Beagle (brown ale, January through March release, 5.4% ABV, 18 IBU), and Juicy Bunny (pale ale, April through June release, 6.2% ABV, 50 IBU).
- "Limited," which in past years included Illudium (barrel-aged old ale, January release, 11.5% ABV), Hellfire (Belgian quadrupel, February release, 10% ABV), Rocket City Red (Irish red ale, St.

Patrick's Day release, 5% ABV), Bourbon Laika (barrel-aged Russian imperial stout, March release, 11.7% ABV), Monkey's Uncle (imperial IPA, March and September release, 8.0% ABV), Hell or Rye Water (rye pale ale, April release, 6.2% ABV), Cabernet Laika (barrel-aged Russian imperial stout, April release, 6.2% ABV), STA 4 (imperial red ale, April release, 8.0% ABV), Gorillanaut (imperial IPA, May release, 10.1% ABV), Vern's (wheat wine ale, May release, 11.0% ABV), ISS Rum (barrel-aged saison, June release, 8.25% ABV), ISS Tequila (barrel-aged saison, July release, 8.25% ABV), ISS Chard (barrel-aged saison, August release, 8.25% ABV), Redstone (Oktoberfest, September release, 6% ABV), Olde Towne (pumpkin ale, September release, 5.0% ABV), Dark Planet (English strong ale, October release, 9.0% ABV), Laika (Russian imperial stout, November release, 11.7% ABV), Black Friday (black IPA, November release, 8.0% ABV), and Unobtanium (barrel-aged old ale, December release, 11.5% ABV).

In case you aren't a space geek, Laika is the name of the dog the Russians sent into space in 1957; ISS stands for International Space Station (or saison); and Monkeynaut is named in honor of Miss Daisy and the other monkeys who helped NASA pave the way for manned spaceflight.

AROUND THE STATE

Good People Brewing, Birmingham

Don't have time to make it to the Good People Brewing taproom? No problem. The good people at Good People have your back. Now you don't even have to leave the Birmingham-Shuttlesworth International Airport; just fly in and step into their Airport Pub. All of the food is carefully paired with handcrafted ales prepared by, you guessed it, the good people of Good People. (Say that three times quickly. I promise it will make you smile.) They offer five year-round beers, four seasonals, and from time to time a special release.

The United States of Craft Beer

Yellowhammer Brewing, Huntsville

A newcomer to the world of craft beers, Yellowhammer arrived on the scene in 2010 with a thunderclap. The brewers focus on Belgian- and German-style beers, but they do it with a Southern twist. For example, their Yellowhammer White is brewed with kaffir lime and a touch of ginger—just enough spice to remind you that you're no longer in the north, Yankee. Their beers are on tap in restaurants and taverns across Alabama, and their most popular styles are also available in 22-ounce bottles.

Alabama

➡ State capital: Montgomery

➡ Alabama trails only Alaska for the highest tax rate on beer in the nation.

➡ There are 21,660 people employed in Alabama in the brewing industry, and the total economic impact from the brewing industry amounts to over $1.9 billion.

➡ Alabama leads the nation in its percentage of restaurants that are classified as "BBQ," and takes third place in barbecue joints per capita.

➡ There are 3.5 million persons of legal drinking age in the state, the average one of whom consumes 30.2 gallons of beer annually.

ALASKA

Alaskan Brewing Company, Juneau

ORIGIN

The Alaskan Brewing Company was founded in 1986 by Marcy and Geoff Larson. It was the first brewery in Juneau, Alaska, since that dark period known as Prohibition. Geoff was a chemical engineer by training and started home brewing in 1979—the same year he met Marcy.

The Larsons' first beer was Alaskan Amber (a delicious beer that is a staple in many pubs and bottle shops). It was brewed from a recipe that dates back to 1907 and that originated in the state of Alaska. They researched other gold rush–era recipes, as well as discovered the ingredients used by Captain Cook—who explored the coast of Alaska in 1777—to brew his beer aboard his ship. It turns out the famous brewing captain used spruce tips in his beer, both as a flavoring and as a way to help ward off scurvy among his sailors. Today, Alaskan Brewing Company uses Alaskan spruce tips to flavor its winter ale.

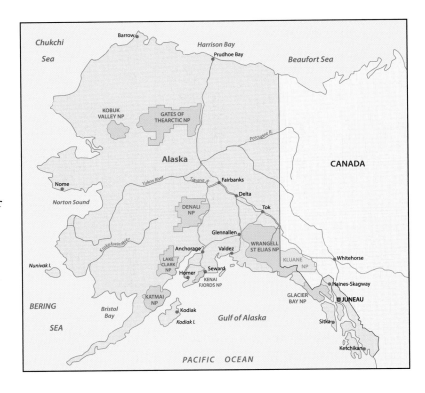

WHY THEY ARE ON TOP

It's not just any one beer that puts Alaskan among the best in the nation. The Larsons' focus, from their first beer to their last, is on preserving and enhancing the history and magnificence of brewing in the state of Alaska. Their recipes use local ingredients whenever possible, and they produce a product that is clearly first a labor of love and second, a commodity to be sold. When it comes to food, beer, wine, or anything that must be savored to be enjoyed, this is always the factor that separates the best from the rest. Without the passion, the love, the creativity to deliver an experience in addition to a taste, the flavor will fall flat.

Nothing flat here.

Alaskan produces six year-round beers: Alaskan Amber (its first beer), Alaskan White (flavored with coriander and orange peels), Alaskan Icy Bay IPA (dry hopped), Alaskan Stout (dark as the night), Alaskan Freeride APA (American pale ale), and Hopothermia (double IPA). It has three seasonals—Alaskan Summer Ale, Alaskan Winter Ale, and Alaskan ESB.

There's also its Pilot Series—a collection of rotating beers that the brewers test in their ten-barrel pilot brewhouse. Each recipe is first put out as a "Rough Draft" before being perfected and eventually released as part of this series in 22-ounce bottles.

Of course, if you are a long-term fan of Alaskan Brewing, you have tried or heard of the company's Smoked Porter. Put out in limited quantities each year on November 1, this beer is a real treat. The bottles proudly display their vintage, like a bottle of wine. And like a wine, Alaskan Smoked Porter can be aged, growing slowly more subtle and interesting over time. If you have a place where you can safely store a bottle or a case, someplace where the temperature is relatively low and does not fluctuate much from day to day, it is worth your time to hole away some of this beer. It will easily hold three to five years, and perhaps longer if the conditions are right. Dust off a bottle each year, and try it against Alaskan's latest release. At the very least, it will be a good excuse to drink a couple of good beers.

One sip of the Smoked Porter and this one needs no explanation. The brewers smoke their malt over alderwood in small batches using a commercial food smoker (think Alaskan smoked salmon, only as a beer and without any fishy taste). This beer also originates from a recipe that is more than 100 years old.

AROUND THE STATE

Anchorage Brewing Company, Anchorage

Started in 2010 by brewer Gabe Fletcher, Anchorage Brewing Company is one of the newest breweries in the nation's northernmost state. It's also one of the smallest, currently putting out only five beers. But what it lacks in sheer numbers, it makes up for in punch. Anchorage's beers are big and bold, offering 22-ounce bottles with corks on top and thick, luscious, barrel-aged elixirs of life inside.

Midnight Sun Brewing Company, Anchorage

Started in 1995, Midnight Sun Brewing brews a variety of year-round beers, as well as a host of seasonals and unique releases. Its beers are offered in 22-ounce bottles and 12-ounce cans in Alaska, Washington, Idaho, Oregon, California, and New York and on tap at the Loft, the brewery's tap-room/pub located at the brewery itself. Every Thursday at 6 p.m., Gary Busse, the owner of the brewery, gives a free tour of the facility.

Alaska

➡ State capital: Juneau

➡ The total annual economic impact of Alaska's brewing industry amounts to just over $475 million, and the industry employs 4,460 people.

➡ Alaskans aren't particularly big soccer fans. The state's inhabitants rank thirty-fifth in their love of the game the rest of the world calls football. I say, Alaska, I'm with you.

➡ There are 513,000 persons of legal drinking age in the state, the average one of whom consumes 28.7 gallons of beer annually.

ARIZONA

Arizona Wilderness Brewing Company, Gilbert

ORIGIN

Arizona Wilderness Brewing began as a business plan on Kickstarter. The founders were asking their backers to supply them with just $40,000 to get them off the ground. That, along with investments they had already secured, would give them a six-month runway of operation. They offered tiers of investment ranging from $10 all the way up to $5,000. During the crowdfunding process, another investor approached the intrepid brewery entrepreneurs and offered to match the investment in the brewery if the Kickstarter project was successfully funded.

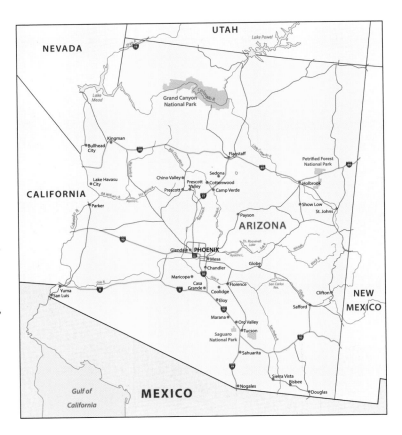

On April 13, 2012, their funding campaign ended with a grand total of $43,414. They got what they needed and another six months of runway to boot. The original business plan forecast the brewery opening in November 2012, but things got pushed back, and the doors didn't officially open until September 2013.

WHY WE LOVE THEM

First and foremost, the three founders of the brewery—Jonathan Buford, Brett Dettler, and Patrick Ware—all have beards. What's not to love about beards? But beyond the beards, these guys are doing some very interesting things with their brews. To say they are shaking things up is only a start. Their Picacho Pecan Pie Brown Ale, for example, was brewed using six whole pecan pies.

Listening to them talk about how they approach brewing is a little like listening to a Michelin-starred chef talk about preparing a menu. The ingredients are key. The juxtaposition of flavors is very important. The desire to create something new and not just repeat past successes drives them forward into new areas of experimentation. They come up with their recipes like a songwriter might write music—going out into nature, finding a beautiful vista or sunset, and calling upon their muses to inspire them into action.

The Arizona Wilderness Brewing Company is located in a strip mall, just a short drive south of Phoenix. It's in a rather inconspicuous location, and if you are driving too fast, you might fly right by. On any given day, you can walk in and not know exactly what you are going to find. Perhaps they'll have only three or four beers on tap. Or maybe they will have as many as eight.

As you can imagine with a group this dedicated to creating new and interesting flavors, Buford, Dettler, and Ware don't stick to a set list of beers. Instead, they brew what has inspired them. Again, it's like watching the work of a great chef. The offerings available when you arrive are like the chef's tasting at a fancy restaurant—all fantastic, but not necessarily something that was listed on a menu. They have used cardamom and faro, blood oranges and caraway seeds, and even, as I mentioned before, full pecan pies in their brews. They have cultivated their own, proprietary yeast from a wild strain that one of the founders collected in the wilderness of Arizona, some 8,000 or 9,000 feet above sea level.

We're not the only ones who love them. In January 2014, Arizona Wilderness was named the best new brewery in the world by RateBeer.com. Less than six months from opening their doors, they were thrust into the spotlight of the craft beer world. If you are within driving distance of these guys, do yourself a favor and try them out. You may have to wait to get in the door, but it will be worth it. We have great expectations for these bearded gents. Get ahold of some of their beer if you can.

AROUND THE STATE

Barrio Brewing Company, Tucson

Beers offered at the Barrio Brewing Company include Barrio Blonde, Red Cat Amber, Copperhead Pale Ale, Barrio India Pale Ale, Taylor Jayne's Raspberry Ale (named after the brewer's first daughter), Hefeweisen, Mocha Java Stout, Barrio Blanco (a white IPA), and Barrio Rojo (a Scottish ale).

If you plan a trip to visit the Barrio Brewing Company in Tucson, make your decision before you get there so you can order quickly, and be sure to arrive just before the train comes through. Anytime the train crossing guards near the brewery are down, they offer Barrio Beer Rail Pints, which cost only $3.25 each.

Four Peaks Brewing Company, Tempe

The building in which the Four Peaks brewery is located was built in 1892. It's constructed almost exclusively out of red brick, except for the ceiling, which is made out of wood. Prior to its life as a brewery, the facility was a creamery. Actually, it was two creameries—first the Pacific Creamery, then the Borden Creamery. Now it's a brewery and brewpub. While I'm a fan of cream

and the things you can make with it, as well as a fan of cows—the original residents of the building—I must say that having a brewery in its place is a big improvement.

Arizona

➡ State capital: Phoenix

➡ The official Arizona State flower is the saguaro cactus blossom, which blooms at the top of the saguaro cactus in May and June.

➡ The most abundant mineral in the state is copper, and the amount used to make the roof of the capitol building in Phoenix is the equivalent of 4,800,000 pennies.

➡ There are 4.7 million persons of legal drinking age in Arizona, the average one of whom consumes 29.5 gallons of beer annually.

ARKANSAS

Diamond Bear Brewing Company, North Little Rock

⭐ ORIGIN

Diamond Bear Brewing was created out of need. The city of Little Rock was without a production brewery, and had been so deprived for more than a dozen years. So, in September 2000, the Bear started brewing. Less than a month later, it started distributing its beer to a single local establishment in the River Market District of Little Rock. In March 2009, with the help of a local economic development commission, the owners doubled their production facility, and they have been going strong ever since.

The brewery got its name from two facts. Though today Arkansas is officially nicknamed the Natural State due to its abundance of forests, pure streams, and wilderness, it's had at least eight different

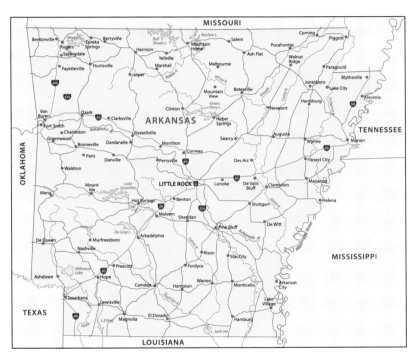

nicknames down through the years. The earliest of these was the Bear State. Thus the "bear" in Diamond Bear. The gemstone part comes from the fact that Arkansas is the only known location in the United States for naturally occurring diamonds—thus the name Diamond Bear was born.

WHY THEY ARE AMONG THE BEST

Russ Melton, one of the founders of Diamond Bear, served in the American military, stationed in Germany for four years. During that time, he learned a lot about beer and brought the love of brewing back home with him when he returned. Today, Diamond Bear employs many European brewing methods when constructing their beers, and everything they produce conforms to the Reinheitsgebot—the Bavarian Purity Law of 1487—which specifies that the only three ingredients allowed in the production of beer are hops, barley, and water (this was before anyone really knew

about the science of yeast). It's one of the oldest consumer protection laws ever created, and though it has been replaced by newer legislation, there are few who would disagree that its creation was one of the most significant moments in the history of beer making.

It's this dedication to a way of beer making and adherence to a law that is now more than 500 years old that makes Diamond Bear a great brewery. That and their desire to not only fill Arkansas with good beer, but share it with the rest of us as well.

Diamond Bear offers five year-round beers and five they release seasonally. The year-round releases are: Pale Ale (6.2% ABV, 33 IBU), Paradise Porter (6.2% ABV, 38 IBU), Presidential IPA (6.2% ABV, 57 IBU), Southern Blonde (5.2% ABV, 22 IBU), and Two Term (double IPA, 8.5% ABV, 90 IBU). Their seasonal releases are: Honey Weiss (summer release, 5.3% ABV, 21 IBU), Irish Red (spring release, 5.8% ABV, 31 IBU), Rocktoberfest (fall release, 5.9% ABV, 32 IBU), Strawberry Blonde (summer release, 5.2% ABV, 20 IBU), and Dogtown Brown (winter release, 5.0% ABV, 25 IBU).

BEER OF ARKANSAS

DIAMOND BEAR BREWING CO.

AROUND THE STATE

■ Stone's Throw Brewing, Little Rock

You might call Stone's Throw Brewing a home-brew club on steroids—the four founders met at their local club while pursuing their hobby. Or, you might call them, as they refer to themselves, "Arkansas's newest nano-brewery." But just because they are small doesn't mean that they aren't mighty. Their taproom has eight taps, which feature exclusive releases, and beer lovers can find their products on tap in numerous locations throughout Little Rock. The flavors and styles change regularly, based on the whims of the brewers and what ingredients happen to be fresh or in season. They frequently schedule beer dinners where they pair their brews with the fare of local restaurants and chefs.

■ Saddlebock Brewery, Springdale

The story of Saddlebock is a tale of love. Steve Rehbock, the brewery's founder and brewmaster, loves beer, as I'm sure you can imagine. Many years ago, when Steve would travel for work or pleasure, he found that he was able to lay his hands on a wealth of craft beer, but each time when he returned to Arkansas, he found himself with limited beer-drinking options. This made Steve sad, and so he decided it was time to learn to home brew. As it turns out, he was quite good at it, and his craft-beer-thirsty friends would come over to his home on a regular basis to partake of his wonderful elixirs. His beer became so popular, in fact, that he decided it was time to start an actual brewery. Clutching his dreams to his chest, Steve approached his wife, Carolyn, about setting aside some space on her horse farm so that he could brew beer. It is due to the love of a wife for her husband that we are now graced with the pleasure of Saddlebock beers—a fairy-tale ending if ever there was one.

Arkansas

➡ State capital: Little Rock

➡ Arkansas has seventy-five counties, and about half of them are dry—meaning you can't purchase alcohol there.

➡ In 2010, there were only three breweries in Arkansas. Today, there are nearly five times that.

➡ It is legal to shoot a bear in Arkansas during a hunt; however, if you try to wake one up just to take a photograph, you will be breaking the law.

➡ There are 2.1 million persons of legal drinking age in the state, the average one of whom consumes 26.7 gallons of beer annually.

CALIFORNIA

AleSmith Brewing Company, San Diego

ORIGIN

AleSmith was originally founded in 1995 by Ted Newcomb and Skip Virgillio, but is currently owned and operated by Peter Zien, AleSmith's brewmaster, who acquired the operation in 2002. The brewery has tripled in size since its inception and moved into a new 105,000–square-foot facility (more than five times larger than its previous site) in early 2015. The new brewery made plans to have an area for food trucks to park and feed the thirsty masses, as well as a cellar for aging beer, and all new brewing equipment. The move should allow AleSmith to gradually increase its production tenfold, from its current 15,000 barrels a year to a whopping 150,000.

WHY WE LOVE THEM

Their beers are diverse and powerful, leaning heavily toward the Belgian style of beer making. The majority of their beers are available in 22-ounce or 750-milliliter bottles, but several are only available in pints or growlers at the taproom.

Their year-round releases include Anvil ESB (5.5% ABV, 30 IBU), Grand Cru (a strong Belgian ale with a foil-wrapped top, 10.0% ABV, 17 IBU), Horny Devil (a Belgian golden ale, 10.0% ABV, 25 IBU), IPA (7.25% ABV, 73 IBU), Lil Devil (a Belgian pale ale, 5.75% ABV, 24 IBU), Nut Brown Ale (5.0% ABV, 17 IBU), Old Numbskull (an American barleywine, 11.0% ABV, 96 IBU), Speedway Stout (12.0% ABV, 70 IBU), Wee Heavy (a Scotch ale, 10.0% ABV, 26 IBU), and X-Extra Pale Ale (5.25% ABV, 35 IBU).

As you can see, they aren't shy about making strong beer. While session beers (those beers brewed to be under 4.0% alcohol so you can throw back a few but still go back to the ammunition factory to work the next day) are nice for those of us not wanting to get completely blasted, there is a lot to be said for the depth and character that bigger beers bring to the table.

Their seasonal beers are also not shy. They are Decadence Anniversary Ale (a special beer brewed first in 2005 to commemorate the brewery's tenth anniversary and now brewed in a different style every year), Evil Dead Red (a deeply red beer brewed each Halloween, 6.66% ABV, 10 IBU), My Bloody Valentine (an American amber ale available in January/February, 6.66% ABV, 10 IBU), Olde Ale (released in spring, 11.0% ABV, 25 IBU), Summer Yule-Smith (a double IPA available in July and August, 8.5% ABV, 105 IBU), and Winter YuleSmith (an American amber ale available for the holidays, 8.5% ABV, 48 IBU).

AleSmith also barrel-ages many of their beers: Grand Cru, Old Numbskull, Speedway Stout, and Wee Heavy. Their Barrel-Aged Speedway Stout was once named the number one beer in the world on RateBeer.com. At the time, that prestige had never been achieved by a North American beer. It's aged for more than nine months in oak barrels, which of course adds flavors of wood and vanilla to the wondrously dark liquid. It's one of their rarest offerings and at one point could only be purchased in pints and growlers at the taproom, but is now available in limited quantities in foil-topped bottles.

Surely the fact that the brewery has twice been named the number one brewer in the world by RateBeer.com is another reason to include AleSmith among the breweries in *The United States of Craft Beer, Updated Edition*. But what really does it for me and puts this brewery among the best is the depth and character of the beers the brewers create. I like to open a beer a little colder than its recommended serving temperature and give it a taste. I like to sip and savor it, enjoying the changes it goes through as it warms to room temperature, revealing subtleties and new layers. It's an exploration and adventure that the brewer guides us through. With AleSmith, this adventure is long and winding. The path twists and turns as new tastes appear over time, adding layers of malt, chocolate, or spice that come out under the crisp citrus or pine of the hops. A well-built beer is something in which you can get lost. Ale-Smith crafts some of the best adventures ever put in bottles.

AROUND THE STATE

Russian River Brewing Company, Santa Rosa

The Russian River Brewing Company, set, like so many of the other great breweries in California, against a backdrop of wineries and grapevines, was originally opened in 1997 by Korbel Champagne Cellars. The vintners wanted to try their hand at brewing beer, and so they hired Vinnie Cilurzo to be their brewmaster. Vinnie was the inventor of the double IPA while he was serving as the brewmaster for another brewery further south, in Temecula. Korbel eventually decided to get out of the beer business, and sold the brewery to Vinnie in 2002. The company expanded their operation in 2004, and later moved to what has become the home of the Russian River Brewing Company at their current facility in Santa Rosa.

Bear Republic Brewing Company, Cloverdale

Brewing beer in the heart of wine country, Bear Republic was founded in 1995 in the middle of Sonoma County. You can still visit their original brewpub, which offers fourteen beers on tap, great food, and a fantastic view of one of the most scenic

parts of California. In keeping with their heritage and love of Sonoma, in 2006, they opened their production brewery, just fifteen miles from the pub. Their beers are big, bold, and hoppy. (There is a reason for the term "West Coast IPA.") They offer eight year-round brews, four seasonals, somewhere in the vicinity of twenty specialty beers, and a handful of barrel-aged beers. In 2014, Bear Republic was recognized as the thirty-sixth-largest craft brewer in the United States. If you haven't tried Racer 5 or Hop Rod Rye, then you are missing out.

Firestone Walker Brewing Company, Paso Robles

Firestone Walker was started in 1996 by Adam Firestone and David

Walker—brothers-in-law who had a passion for good beer. Located in California's Central Coast, a region whose name evokes images of vineyards and wineglasses but upon closer inspection should perhaps be as well known for hoppy beers and pint glasses, the brewery has long been renowned for its pale ales. The brewers offer four beers in their Lion and Bear series (based on the nicknames of the two founders), three seasonals, and three eclectic brews in their Proprietor's Reserve series. In addition, they release a Proprietor's Vintage series of limited barrel-aged beers and a large handful of experimental beers from the Barrelworks.

Stone Brewing Company, Escondido

Stone Brewing was founded in 1996 by Greg Koch and Steve Wagner. Their first release occurred that same year. The beer? Stone Pale Ale. A year later, their iconic Arrogant Bastard Ale made its debut. That first year, they brewed just 400 barrels of beer. In 2013, they put out more than 213,000, making Stone one of the fastest-growing breweries in the nation. That may seem like meteoric growth, and well, yes it is. But I for one welcome our new beer overlords. World domination cannot come fast enough. Their beers are hop-heavy monsters—with teeth and claws—that will growl at you until you take notice. They are delicious and wonderful, and should be sent to every corner of the earth to liberate those who have never known what it means to be freed from the oppressiveness of watery, tasteless beer.

California

➡ State capital: Sacramento

➡ There are more than 450 working breweries in California, more than any other state.

➡ The state is the third-largest producer of beer in the United States, but the largest producer of craft beer, brewing somewhere in the vicinity of 2.9 million barrels of handcrafted beer each year.

➡ The craft brewing industry in California employs over 44,000 people, paying out wages that amount to more than $1.7 billion.

➡ There are 27 million persons of legal drinking age in the state, the average one of whom consumes 25.5 gallons of beer annually.

COLORADO

Oskar Blues Brewery, Longmont

ORIGIN

Oskar Blues made its world debut as Oskar Blues Grill and Brew Restaurant. That was in Lyons, Colorado, and the year was 1997. In 1998, they brewed their first batch of beer in the basement of the restaurant. In the same year they took home a bronze medal from the Great American Beer Festival for their entry called The Reverend Sandi's Sinful Stout. In 2002, they became the first US craft brewery to offer their beer in cans, releasing their hoppy ambrosia known as Dale's Pale Ale. Their first canning "line," if you can call it that, could handle only one can at a time, and was operated by hand. In 2008, they moved into a 35,000-square-foot facility

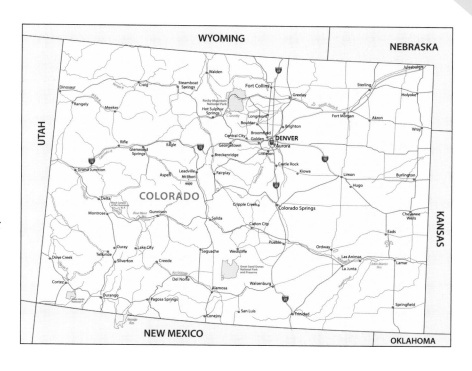

in Longmont, which included a new canning line that could put out 160 cans *per minute*—and was no longer operated by hand. In 2012, they expanded again, increasing their production capacity to 100,000 barrels and installing an even faster can line that almost doubled their output, now reaching 300 cans a minute.

WHY THEY ARE AMONG THE BEST

All Oskar Blues beers are released in cans. The company lines the inside with a protective coating so that there is no reaction between the suds and the metal of the can. Unlike glass bottles, cans don't let any light in, so the beer is protected from sun damage during transportation or while it's on display. Additionally, cans can be filled nearly all the way to the top, meaning there is less oxygen inside with the beer, meaning that the beer breaks down more slowly, and stays fresh longer. Perhaps best of all, the metal of the cans is more conductive than glass, so your beers will get cold faster when dropped in a cooler of ice or just resting in the fridge.

Unlike some craft brewers, Oskar Blues doesn't offer a page-long list of different releases, but what they do put out is out of this world. They have five year-round releases, two seasonals, and three special releases—one of which is a root beer and another of which is a collaboration with Sun King Brewing Company.

Their flagship brand, Dale's Pale Ale (6.5% ABV, 65 IBU) has a fantastic malt backbone, which sits up straight and tall as it supports a delicious bouquet of citrusy, floral hops. It can be purchased in 12-ounce cans, 19.2-ounce cans (known as a "stovepipe"), ⅙ barrel, and ½ barrel. Mama's Little Yella Pils (5.3% ABV, 35 IBU), their craft beer version of the popular Czech-style beer, is lighter and comes with an easier-to-swallow alcohol percentage, but still packs a nice wallop of hops. Nice for a warm summer day, it's also available in 12-ounce, 19.2-ounce, ⅙ barrel, and ½ barrel sizes. Old Chub, their Scotch ale (8.0% ABV), is slightly more viscous than their other beers, but it's surprisingly easy to drink and has been known to turn even light beer drinkers to the dark side. Old Chub is available in all sizes except the stovepipe. Their Deviant Dale's IPA (8.0% ABV, 85 IBU) is a massive, hulking beer with an extra dose of piney, sticky, citrusy hops that clings like resin to the coppery red malt structure, which seems miles thick.

It's available in 16-ounce "big ones," ⅙ barrels, and ½ barrels. The last of their year-round releases, G'Knight (8.7% ABV, 60 IBU) was once called Gordon, but, like a rap star, had a name-ectomy in 2011, which added the title of nobility and apostrophe, changing its name but not the delicious magic inside.

Oskar Blues beers have become one of the standard-bearers for the craft beer industry in America. They are consistent, delicious, big and bold, and often easy to locate. Even when I'm tempted to explore beers from new breweries, if I see an Oskar Blues on the menu, I find myself irresistibly drawn back into the fold. The flavors are classics—comforting and familiar and perfectly executed. Having grown up in a world that once thought of all beer in cans as thin, pale, inferior brew, I find great pleasure in popping one open and sipping something so magnificent from a vessel with so little pretension.

★ AROUND THE STATE

Ska Brewing, Durango

Ska Brewing got its name from the founders' love of, as you might imagine, ska music. Ska has been described as the upbeat, bass-rhythm-heavy precursor to reggae. It was created sometime in the late 1950s and was itself influenced by calypso music and American jazz. This funky, offbeat music is a great analogy for the brewery itself. The website looks like it sprang fully formed off the pages of a mad cartoonist's sketchbook. Their facility is powered by 100 percent wind, the walls are insulated with recycled blue jeans, and the tables and bar are made from salvaged bowling alleys. Stuck right smack dab in the middle of this eclectic yet strangely elegant menagerie is their beer—brewed with heart, passion, and soul.

Left Hand Brewing Company, Longmont

The Left Hand Brewing Company was started in September 1993—well, sort of. The company, founded by Dick Doore and Eric Wallace, was originally named Indian Peaks Brewing Company, an homage to the Indian Peaks Wilderness, which is nearby the brewery. However, just before they were about to release their first batch of beer, they discovered that another brewery was using the name Indian Peaks for a style of beer they were producing. Not wanting to confuse consumers, and not interested in a legal battle over the name, they quickly changed the name of the brewery. After some deliberation, they decided to name the company after Chief Niwot, who led his tribe to camp in the area during the winters. *Niwot* is a southern Arapahoe word that means, you guessed it, "left hand."

Great Divide Brewing Company, Denver

Prior to creating the Great Divide Brewing Company, Brian Dunn, the founder, spent five years abroad, helping to build farms in developing countries. When he returned to Colorado, he went to graduate school and learned to home brew. In 1993, he started his professional brewing odyssey, launching into what would prove to be a very decorated craft beer career. Great Divide has brought home eighteen Great American Beer Festival awards, five World Beer Cup awards, and was named number seven on BeerAdvocate.com's All-Time Top Brews List of 2010.

Next Stop Brew Co., Denver

Previously brewing under the longer, yet still cool name of Intrepid Sojourner Beer Project, Next Stop offers up brews inspired by international cuisine. The names of their beers sound like an itinerary for someone on a round-the-world tour—Amsterdam, Rome, Bangkok, Istanbul… And like the names, the flavors themselves are off the beaten path. Care for a basil IPA? Or a Turkish coffee stout? How about a lemongrass and ginger Kölsch?

Colorado

➡ State capital: Denver

➡ Colorado has 175 craft breweries and produces 1.4 million barrels of craft beer per year.

➡ Drinking alcohol at higher elevations will get you drunk faster. Drinking in Denver, known as the "Mile-High City," will help you get your buzz on faster than in most other cities in America.

➡ The Great American Beer Festival, or GABF, takes place each year in Colorado. It is the largest and most highly renowned festival in the United States and gives out medals for beers submitted in every category you could possibly imagine. According to the *Guinness Book of World Records*, there is no other place on earth where you can find more beers on tap at one time than at the GABF.

➡ There are 3.7 million persons of legal drinking age in the state, the average one of whom consumes 30.0 gallons of beer annually.

CONNECTICUT

New England Brewing Company, Woodbridge

⭐ ORIGIN

New England Brewing started in 2003 and is currently headed up by founding brewer Rob Leonard. Rob has more than twenty years of professional brewing under his belt. He started in 1992 at New Haven Brewing Company, working his way up from the lowly rank of assistant all the way to head brewer. But great beer is seldom made by just one man, and such is the case at New England Brewing. The other key members of the team include Matt Westfall, one-time intern, now partner and head brewer; Bill Pastyrnak, CEO and partner; James, who needs no introduction or title; Hospitality Gorilla; and Eli the Dog, head of security.

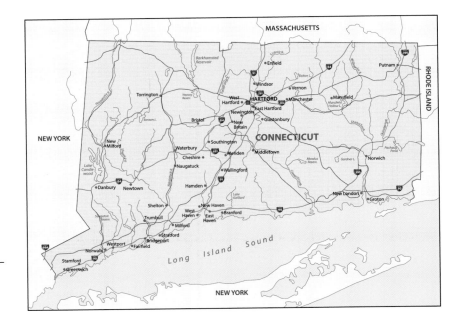

The United States of Craft Beer

WHY THEY ARE AMONG THE BEST

It's not just the fact that New England Brewing has no fewer than nine different renderings of Elvis inside their brewery that makes us like them. They are also only the second brewer on the East Coast to release their beer in cans, adding their considerable voice to the growing cacophony of those advocating craft beer in cans. In addition to being lighter and more compact than bottles—which makes cans easier and cheaper to ship and store—cans are also reputed to be better at protecting the beer inside from outside elements, like light and oxygen.

The fact that the company has a framed "cease and desist" order on the wall of the brewery—from none other than George Lucas—doesn't hurt their case for being well liked. As it turns out, the original art on their Imperial Stout Trooper looked like a Storm Trooper. This, of course, upset George and his lawyers, and so the brewery received the letter. In the end, they added a pair of sunglasses to the trooper on the can, and, well, problem solved.

The artwork on their other products is also entertaining. Their Gandhi-Bot (double IPA) has a picture of a robot with the features of the peace-inspiring Mahatma Gandhi, doling out love and

understanding with generous tastes of his hop-infused serum of self-purification and truth. And their 668 The Neighbor of the Beast (Belgian-style ale) depicts a suburban home, complete with white picket fence and a blood-red silhouette of the huge horn-adorned head of "the Beast," who clearly lives next door. By the way, the blurb on the can says, "Good fences make good neighbors—unless you live next door to Satan. Then you may need a little something extra to help you cope."

New England Brewing Company offers a number of different styles in cans, large bottles, and on draft. When it comes right down to it, Elvis and an angry George Lucas are great, but we want good beer, man. New England Brewing has it—by the canful.

AROUND THE STATE

Stubborn Beauty Brewing Company, Middletown

Stubborn Beauty Brewing Company had an unusually usual start. Craft brewers beginning as home brewers is a tale we have heard before. However, the founders' repeated history of submitting their beers to contests and coming out near the top is quite extraordinary. They made their first batch in February 2009. It was an imperial IPA, which they named after the noises they made while drinking it—Nummy Nummy. Later that year, they competed in the best-in-show portion of the HomeBrewTalk.com home-brewing contest. They took third place out of more than 300 entries with an imperial porter, which they called Porter Justice. In 2010, they entered the Samuel Adams Longshot Homebrew and again came home with an impressive score. In 2011, they came full circle, competing again in the HomeBrewTalk.com contest, but this time coming home in the top spot. Their beers are available only at the brewery. Bring your own growler or buy one there. But whatever you do, don't forget a lid!

Thomas Hooker Brewing Company, Bloomfield

The namesake of the brewery, Thomas Hooker, was born in Leicestershire, England. He was a reverend, a puritan, and a pilgrim. He moved from his home in England to Holland, and eventually to New England, where he is credited as the founder of Hartford, Connecticut. Like its namesake, Thomas Hooker Brewing is a pioneer. The company brings creativity, vision, and above all else, bravery in the name of progress. They make beers that are bold, solid, and unafraid of the unknown—beers unique enough to be the backbone of a community, strong enough to help forge a nation.

Connecticut

➡ State capital: Hartford

➡ Connecticut was the fifth state to join the Union, formally becoming part of the United States on January 9, 1788.

➡ The official state shellfish is the Eastern oyster, which would be quite tasty with a pint of Connecticut-brewed stout or porter.

➡ There are 2.6 million persons of legal drinking age in the state, the average one of whom consumes 22.0 gallons of beer annually.

DELAWARE

Dogfish Head Brewery, Milton

⭐ ORIGIN

Opened in 1995, Dogfish Head was Delaware's first brewpub. Their first batch of beer—Shelter Pale Ale—was brewed in batches of just 12 gallons at a time. The tiny batches and distribution only to their own brewpub made Dogfish Head the country's smallest commercial brewery. The small batches made it easy for them to experiment with new recipes, different flavors, and new ways of approaching traditional beers.

But when you brew your beer 12 gallons at a time, you can only quench the thirst of so many people. Within a year Dogfish Head had expanded, not once but twice—the first expansion adding thirty times the brewing capacity. By 1999, they had five year-round bottled beers and had expanded into almost a dozen states. By 2008 they had outgrown a fifty-barrel brewing system, which they sold to the Russian River Brewing Company in northern California.

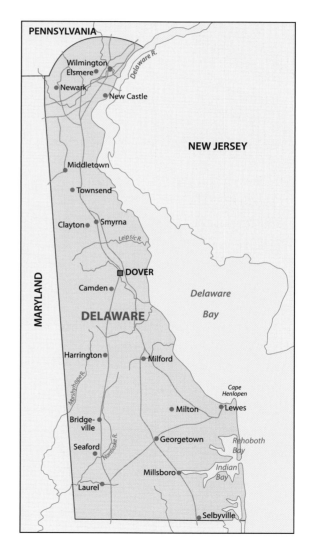

WHY THEY TOP THE LIST

Today Dogfish Head operates out of a 100,000-square-foot facility, offers more than twenty different types of beer, and is distributed to more than half the states in the Union. Despite their growth and success, the inventiveness and fearless creativity that was born out of that 12-gallon brewing station hasn't left the brewery. They continue to try new things and deliver surprising new flavors for beer lovers to savor and search for.

For example, in 1999, Dogfish Head created a beer that was based on a recipe discovered in Turkey, inside the tomb of King Midas—named, appropriately, Midas Touch. The recipe was based on ingredients found in a drinking vessel that was more than 2,700 years old. Somewhere between wine and mead, this brew is thick and sweet and might even be described as viscous and sticky.

Then, in 2001, Dogfish Head introduced us to their 90 Minute IPA—a malty, hoppy, delicious brew that is continuously hopped for a full ninety minutes during the brewing process. Two different oils that come from the hop plant are beneficial for beer brewing. One adds flavor to the beer, the other aroma. The flavor is often

described as citrusy, piney, or simply bitter, and the aroma follows what you would expect from those flavors. But these two oils come out of the hop plant at different temperatures, so traditionally, brewers will add hops to their brews at two different points during the process.

Dogfish Head's brewers decided they would try adding hops to the boiling wort continuously, bridging the gap between the two hop additions. To do this, they used one of those old vibrating football games—the ones where you set up a play by placing your little men on the playing field, then turning on the board, making it vibrate and sending the little metal players scattering. The brewers placed the hops on the vibrating table and let them slowly scatter into the brew for a full ninety minutes. The results were so successful that they added a 60 Minute IPA, a 120 Minute IPA, and have even created a 75 Minute IPA, which is a cask-conditioned blend of 60 Minute and 90 Minute.

In 2003, brewery founder and president Sam Calagione, along with Dogfish Head brewer Bryan Selders, recorded a hip-hop album. The duo call themselves the Pain Relievaz. Once you've knocked back a few of their beers, you can look them up on *YouTube*. Their beer is great and adds significant value to the experience of watching their videos.

AROUND THE STATE

Crooked Hammock Brewery, Lewes and Middletown

The folks at Crooked Hammock brew their beers to fit a simple philosophy—that at the end of a long, hard day, it's time to kick back, relax, and have a beer to unwind. Their beers are easy to drink, and pair well with comfort foods, flip-flops, shorts, and the things in life that get you through that tough day. If you can't escape to the beach, then escape to your own backyard.

Fordham & Dominion Brewing Company, Dover

Fordham & Dominion Brewing Company is a two-headed monster. Not that long ago they were separate entities. Fordham Brewing Company was started in 1995 on the top floor of the Rams Head Tavern in Annapolis. Its founders had to actually take the roof off of the building in order to get the brewing equipment inside. A few years earlier, in 1989, the Old Dominion Brewing Company had set up shop over in Virginia, making and selling craft brews and gourmet soda, which they sold out of their brewpub in the city of Ashburn. The two companies joined forces in 2007 and consolidated their operations in Delaware in 2009.

Delaware

➥ State capital: Dover

➥ Delaware was the first state in the Union—the first to ratify the United States Constitution—on December 7, 1787.

➥ Delaware was settled very early on by the Dutch, who ruled the area from about 1655 to about 1664 and built no fewer than three breweries in the city of New Amstel, now known as New Castle.

➥ There are 672,000 persons of legal drinking age in the state, the average one of whom consumes 33.6 gallons of beer annually.

FLORIDA

Cigar City Brewing, Tampa

★ ORIGIN

The name Cigar City Brewing is derived from the nickname of the city in which it makes its home. Tampa is known by many as the "Cigar City," since there are, in fact, many famous cigar factories there.

Cigar City brewed their first barrel of beer in 2009. They have won a gold and a silver medal at the Great American Beer Festival, and at one point were named the number four brewery in the world by RateBeer.com. In addition to bringing the world great beer, the fine folks at CCB are dedicated to preserving and teaching the history of Tampa. Many of their beers are named after locations and important figures from the city's past—Guava Grove and José Martí, for example.

WHY THEY ARE SO GOOD

The brewers at Cigar City throw plenty of creativity into the vat. Take for example their Cucumber Saison (5.0% ABV, 10 IBU). Available in June, this unusual brew is made to be refreshing and light. The cucumber has the power to cool your tongue—ideal for drinking on hot days in the Florida sun. Or perhaps you'd prefer their Sugar Plum Brown Ale (5.0% ABV, 22 IBU). Available in November, just in time for the Christmas season, this one sports flavors of cinnamon, ginger, cardamom, and rose—the spices of freshly baked sugar-plums to dance in your head before, during, or after a holiday feast.

At the end of the day, it's about fun, about exploration and creativity—bringing something new to the table, trying new ways to enhance traditional recipes to make them unique to Tampa or to Cigar City Brewing. It's these things that are at the heart of the craft beer movement: the search for something new, the quest for new taste, finding something off the beaten path. The brewers at Cigar City Brewing are bringing us the vehicles to get off that path, and that is why we love them.

Cigar City offers eight year-round brews: Jai Alai India Pale Ale (7.5% ABV, 70 IBU), Florida Cracker (Belgian-style white ale, 5.5% ABV, 18 IBU), Invasion (pale ale, 5.0% ABV, 36 IBU), Maduro (brown ale, 5.5% ABV, 25 IBU), Tocobaga (red ale, 7.2% ABV, 75 IBU), Hotter Than Helles (Munich-style lager, 5.0% ABV, 20 IBU), White Oak Jai Alai (a barrel-aged version of their Jai Alai IPA, 7.5% ABV, 70 IBU), and Humidor Series IPA (aged in Spanish cedar, the same wood used to make cigar boxes and fine humidors; 7.5% ABV, 70 IBU).

In addition, Cigar City puts out a very large handful—okay, maybe several handfuls—of seasonal beers. Perhaps the best known of these is Marshal Zhukov's Imperial Stout (11.0% ABV, 80 IBU).

It's named after the Russian general who, during World War II, led the Soviet army against the Axis powers. He was responsible for liberating the Soviet Union from occupying enemy forces and, more importantly, pushing into the heart of Nazi Germany and taking Berlin. He remains today the most decorated general in Russian history. This imperial stout is very dark, almost an oily black, and has flavors of chocolate and molasses. According to the brewery, you should pair Marshal Zhukov's with mushroom dishes, dark chocolate, cherries, and ground wars in Russia.

AROUND THE STATE

▪ *Intracoastal Brewing Company, Melbourne*

Ever have the burning desire to do yoga in a brewery? Me neither, but if, now that I've mentioned it, Downward-Facing Pint seems like something you might be interested in—since, you know, once you finish, you're just an arm's length from the tap handles, just sayin'—then look no further than Intracoastal Brewing Company. In addition to offering their delicious beers in pints, half-pints, flights, and growlers, they also offer yoga classes in their taproom on Sundays between 11:30 a.m. and 1:00 p.m. Classes are $15, and the cost includes your first pint.

Due South Brewing Company, Boynton Beach

The founder of Due South Brewing Company, Mike Halker, wasn't initially a fan of beer. He started his journey into the annals of craft brew history like so many do: with a visit to a local home-brew store. However, he wasn't there to make beer; he was on a mission to make sulfite-free wine for his wife, Jodi. But as it turns out, wine takes a long time to make, and the home-brew store owner was quite persuasive in his defense of beer as a superior beverage. That was in the early 2000s. Due South Brewing Company opened for business in 2012. The rest, as they say, is history.

Florida

➡ State capital: Tallahassee

➡ There are now over seventy operating breweries in Florida.

➡ There are more than 30,000 lakes and over 1,000 golf courses in the state.

➡ The state was named by explorer Ponce de León in 1513. The name *Florida*, translated from the original Spanish, means "covered in flowers."

➡ A large section of the Florida coast has been dubbed the "Space Coast" since both Cape Canaveral and Kennedy Space Center are in the area. This is where many of the US spacecraft have been launched from.

➡ There are 14.6 million persons of legal drinking age in the state, the average one of whom consumes 27.4 gallons of beer annually.

GEORGIA

Terrapin Beer Company, Athens

ORIGIN

The Terrapin Beer Company was founded in 2002 by John Cochran and Brian "Spike" Buckowski. The two men met while working together at the Atlanta Brewing Company. Like many craft beer entrepreneurs, they had beer in their blood—both figuratively and literally. Both had a long-term love affair with home brewing; both made their way into the professional ranks of the brewing industry; and when they found each other, the logical next step was to have a pint and start their own brewery. They set up their operation in Athens, Georgia, naming the company after Brian's favorite Grateful Dead album, *Terrapin Station*.

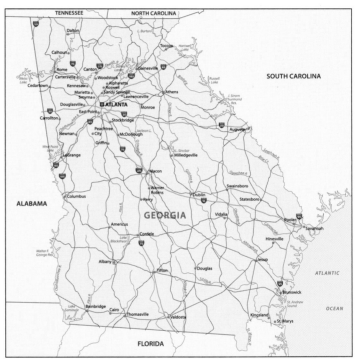

They started out working with contract brewers—hiring other breweries to produce the beer for them in their facilities, which proved to be much less expensive than buying commercial brewing equipment and leasing a space to use it in. The company was quite small at first, making award-winning beer but unable to grow their market substantially without more production power. So in 2006, John and Brian got an $800,000 investment from a group of Athens investors and finally took their brew to the next level, installing their own facility, and setting to it like men on a mission. Their hard work paid off, and in 2008, they moved into a 40,000-square-foot facility, with a 100-barrel brewhouse.

⭐ WHY THEY ROCK

At Terrapin, they consistently put out award-winning product. In 2008, at the Australian International Beer Awards, they won the bronze for their Golden Ale (5.3% ABV, 21 IBU) and the silver for their Wake 'N' Bake Coffee Oatmeal Imperial Stout (8.6% ABV, 50 IBU). That same year they won the Best Beer award at the Atlanta Summer Beer Fest. In 2009, at the Carolina Championship of Beers, their Rye Pale Ale (5.5% ABV, 35 IBU) won a bronze, their Hop Karma IPA (now retired) also won a bronze, and their Sunray Wheat (also retired from rotation) brought home a gold. In 2012, their Easy Rider (also retired) took home the session beer silver medal from the US Open Beer Championship. In 2013, RecreationAle (a hoppy session ale, 4.7% ABV, 42 IBU) came home from the US Open Beer Championship with the bronze, and their Hopzilla (10.7% ABV, 110 IBU!) was named the best imperial IPA in the Mid-Atlantic/Southeast region at the US Open Beer Championship.

In addition to winning awards, the brewers are constantly bringing new flavors and blazing new trails with their beers. They offer six year-round brews, four seasonals, four beers in what they call the Monster Beer Tour, and a mixed case, so to speak, of special releases, "Side Projects," and collaborations with other breweries. The beers range in flavor profiles from lighter session beers to hulking hop monsters to sweet treats—like chocolate peanut butter porter or chili pepper brownie. In the end, the company just puts out good beer, consistently drinkable and often over-the-top funky, but never disappointing.

AROUND THE STATE

SweetWater Brewing Company, Atlanta

The SweetWater brewery officially opened its doors on February 17, 1997, but its story starts much earlier. It starts, in fact, in another town altogether, in a college dorm room. Kevin McNerney and Freddy Bensch, the brewery's founders, were roommates in college in Boulder, Colorado. They both, of course, had a love of beer, and managed to turn this love into jobs—washing out kegs on the loading dock of a local brewery (as the legend goes, they were paid in beer). After graduating from school, the pair decided that their education wasn't complete and left for California to finish their fermentation science degrees at the American Brewers Guild. Heading to Atlanta during the summer Olympics in 1996, they scraped together the cash to set up shop, and the rest, as they say, is history.

◾ *Wild Heaven Craft Beers, Avondale Estates*

Wild Heaven Craft Beers was founded in late 2010. It offers only the finest in high-end beers, producing just six styles: Invocation (Belgian-style golden ale, 8.5% ABV, 48 IBU), Ode to Mercy (imperial brown ale, 8.2% ABV, 40 IBU), Eschaton (Belgian-style quadrupel ale, 10.5% ABV, 20 IBU), Let There Be Light (American pale ale, 4.7% ABV, 30 IBU), White Black-bird (Belgian-style saison, 6.0% ABV, 15.5 IBU), and Civilization (English-style bar-leywine, 12.0% ABV, 40 IBU). They are available throughout Georgia on tap and in four-pack bottles.

Georgia

➥ State capital: Atlanta

➥ Georgia became the fourth state in the United States, entering the Union on January 2, 1788.

➥ It is the eighth most populous state in the nation, weighing in at just about 10 million people.

➥ There are 6.9 million people of legal drinking age in Georgia, the average one of whom consumes 25.7 gallons of beer annually.

HAWAII

Maui Brewing Company, Lahaina

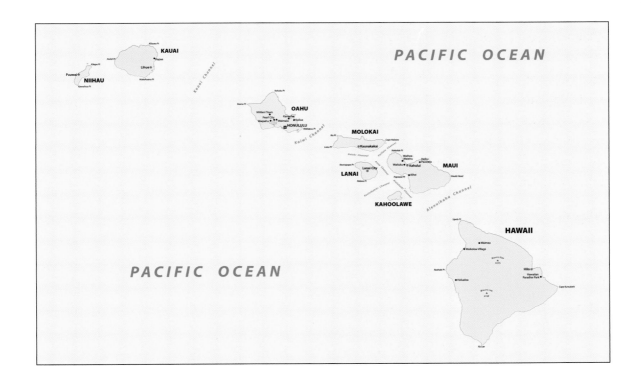

⭐ ORIGIN

The Maui Brewing Company came into existence in 2005, bringing Hawaiian-inspired brews to people across the islands and on the mainland. The beauty, texture, and sweetness of island life is woven into their beers, using items produced in Hawaii as the backbone of their beers—fresh pineapple, honey from Kauai, or even rum distilled in Maui.

WHY THEY STAND OUT

If you've ever been to Hawaii, you know why so many people refer to it as paradise. The air is sweet, the sun seems to always be out, and the beach is always close by. But such beauty comes at a price. The islands are small and depend on imports of many things in order to maintain their economy. The concept of "earth friendly" isn't just a nice idea—it's also a way of life for those who would protect their fragile paradise from being destroyed.

Maui Brewing Company believes in creating as small of a footprint on the islands as possible. To keep paradise looking good, you have to work hard to avoid breaking down the fragile ecosystems that make the islands so beautiful. To that end, all of the brewery's delivery trucks run on biodiesel (vehicle fuel made from biodegradable materials such as vegetable oil or animal fat). All of the brewery's packaging is made from recycled cardboard. The brewery is lighted by high-efficiency, energy-saving light bulbs. And all of the spent yeast, grain, and hops that come out after the brewing process are donated to local Maui farmers to feed to their pigs and cattle.

But the company's dedication to both its beer and protecting its home doesn't stop there. Maui Brewing Company exclusively uses cans to package its beers—not glass. The reasons: Cans are recyclable, are lighter weight (so they require less fuel to transport from the brewery to the store), and cool faster (meaning they use less energy to make them cold).

The company's flagship beers include Bikini Blonde Lager (5.1% ABV, 18 IBU), Big Swell IPA (6.2% ABV, 82 IBU), CoCo-Nut PorTer (6.0% ABV, 30 IBU), and Mana Wheat (5.5% ABV, 18 IBU). They also do limited releases in fall/winter and spring/summer. The brewery has a tasting room, and tours are available on Thursdays, Fridays, and Saturdays.

AROUND THE STATE

Kona Brewing Company, Kailua-Kona

The Kona Brewing Company was started by a father and son team. They bottled their first two brews, Pacific Golden Ale (the name was later changed to Big Wave Golden Ale) and Fire Rock Pale Ale, in 1995. They have since added two beers to their Flagship series—Longboard Island Lager and Castaway IPA—and along with their three Aloha series beers—Koko Brown, Pipeline Porter, and Wailua Wheat—they are distributed in thirty-six states and nine different countries.

Hawaii

➥ State capital: Honolulu

➥ Beer-industry-related jobs: 8,990

➥ Hawaii is ranked thirty-eighth in the United States in number of craft brewers per capita, with a grand total of eight.

➥ Hawaii is the youngest and southernmost state in the Union. It's also the only state that is growing over time, due to continued volcanic eruptions that slowly add to its land mass.

➥ There are 1 million persons of drinking age in the state, the average one of whom consumes 30.4 gallons of beer annually.

IDAHO

Grand Teton Brewing Company, Victor

ORIGIN

Started in 1988 by Charlie and Ernie Otto and originally named Otto Brothers' Brewing Company, Grand Teton was the first microbrewery in Wyoming. In 1989, the brothers stumbled upon an old European lidded bucket, which had been used before the bottle cap was invented. People would bring this bucket to their local pub and have the brewer fill it up with beer to take home. The name of this vessel was the "growler." After rediscovering this remarkable artifact, the Otto brothers reinvented it as a 64-ounce glass jug with a screw top—and the modern growler was born.

In 1998, the brothers broke ground on a new brewery at the base of Teton Pass in Victor, Idaho. This was an ideal place for

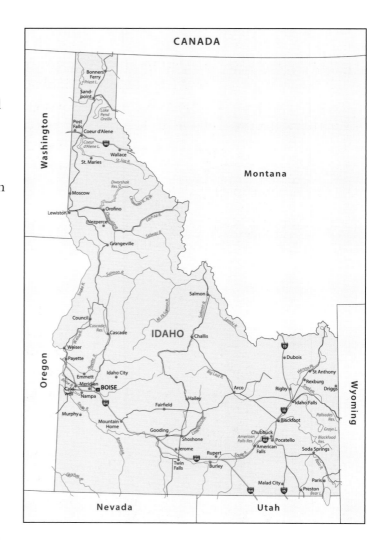

a brewery, since there was an abundance of locally grown barley, Northwest hops, and glacier water nearby. The new brewery allowed them to increase their distribution, expanding out from Idaho into Wyoming, Montana, and Utah. In the fall of 2000, the name was changed to Grand Teton Brewing, and in 2009 the brewery was sold to Steve and Ellen Furbacher.

Grand Teton Brewing Company is the original brewery of Grand Teton and Yellowstone National Park. Situated at the base of the Tetons, it uses only glacial runoff for brewing its delicious beers. The water is naturally filtered through granite and limestone, taking several hundred years to slowly work its way down to the spring where the brewery draws its water, just a half mile from the front door.

The company's current brewing facility is in an 11,000-square-foot building, which houses all of the production and packaging, as well as cold storage, a conditioning area, and, of course, their pub and tasting room. They have a thirty-barrel brewhouse and fermentation tanks in the basement that can hold up to 660 barrels' worth of beer.

WHY THEY ARE ON TOP

Any brewery that can claim to be behind the resurgence of the growler has to be in the running not only for best brewery but also for being a legendary part of American brewing history. More to the point, Grand Teton Brewing Company focuses on the core of beer brewing—what goes into the beer. Like the Bavarians, who loved their beer enough to enact laws to protect its purity, Grand Teton selects only the purest ingredients and water. They make fantastic beer with the freshest ingredients, going so far as to build their brewery in the ideal spot to capitalize on the centuries-long filtration process of Mother Nature. Good product in, good product out. Sometimes it's that simple.

Grand Teton Brewing Company offers six signature brews: Bitch Creek ESB Ale (6.0% ABV, 60 IBU), Sweetgrass APA (American pale ale, 6.0% ABV, 60 IBU), Amber Ale (4.7% ABV, 20 IBU), Howling Wolf Weisse Beer (4.7% ABV, 14 IBU), Old Faithful Ale (pale golden ale, 4.7% ABV, 16 IBU), and Ale 208 (session ale, 4.7% ABV, 16 IBU).

In addition, they offer five seasonals: Trout Hop Black IPA (available January through March, 8.5% ABV, 117 IBU), Lost Continent Double IPA (available April through June, 8.0% ABV, 117 IBU), Snarling Badger Berliner Weisse (available in summertime, 7.5% ABV, 9 IBU), Pursuit of Hoppiness Imperial Red Ale (available October through December, 8.5% ABV, 100 IBU), and Fest Bier Lager (available August 1, 6.0% ABV, 24 IBU).

AROUND THE STATE

Laughing Dog, Ponderay

The yellow Labrador retriever on the label of their beers goes by the name Ben. He's not just a cartoon but a real-life dog. He's been the family dog of Fred and Michelle Colby for quite some time. So long, in fact, that they claim Ben is the one who runs the brewery. Before you go and get your cap in a twist over health regulations and food safety inspections, Ben is not so much a hands-on boss. He's more of an idea dog. He knows if an idea is good or not and will tell his family so—one bark meaning "okay/good," two for "no." Started in 2005, Laughing Dog has released fifteen different beers, several of which are award winners. If you get a chance to visit the little lakeside community of Sandpoint, drop in for a pint. The folks at Laughing Dog don't bite.

Selkirk Abbey Brewing Company, Post Falls

Though you wouldn't think of giving Post Falls, Idaho, the nickname Little Belgium, that didn't stop the folks at Selkirk Abbey from opening up a Belgian-themed brewery there. Though they have been known on occasion to make an American pale ale or a German doppelbock, they are the only craft brewery in Idaho that specializes in Belgian-style beers. Everything from their taproom all the way down to their labels speaks to the dedication they have to their chosen style. The ancient art of beer making has found its home in America's heartland.

Idaho

➥ State capital: Boise

➥ The word *potato* first appeared on an Idaho license plate in 1928, but it wasn't until 1957 that the slogan "Famous Potatoes" made its debut—and it's still there today.

➥ The statehouse in the capital of Boise is entirely heated geothermally from underground hot springs.

➥ Idaho is 83,557 square miles, of which 63 percent is public land, and has 3,100 miles of river—more river miles than any other state.

➥ There are 1.1 million persons of legal drinking age in the state, the average one of whom consumes 27.8 gallons of beer each year.

ILLINOIS

Revolution Brewing, Chicago

ORIGIN

Revolution Brewing officially opened its doors in February 2010, but the company's story begins much earlier. Managing partner Josh Deth started his journey down the craft brew road as a home brewer. In 1995, he broke into the industry professionally, washing out kegs for Golden Prairie Brewing, an operation that is sadly no longer with us. Josh worked his way up through the industry, eventually finding his way to Goose Island Beer Company as a cellarman and brewpub brewer. It was while working at Goose Island that he had the idea for Revolution.

Finally, in 2003, after a few failed attempts, Josh, his wife Krista, and a handful of friends opened Handlebar, a restaurant and bar in Wicker Park. Though they were in the food business, the idea of a full-blown brewery was still rattling around in the back of Josh's mind. It took him nearly three years to wrangle the investment and permits necessary to get the operation off the ground, but eventually it

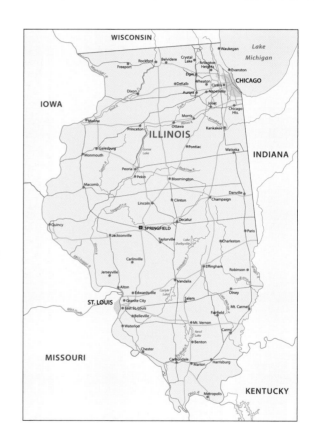

all came together. The brewery has grown every year since its inception, adding a second-floor beer lounge in 2011 and a full production brewery and taproom in 2012.

WHY THEY ARE SO GOOD

Most of Revolution Brewing's beer labels have either a little red star, the internationally recognized symbol of the revolutionary, or a clenched fist, the internationally recognized sign for I'll Punch You If You Don't Try My Beer. My favorite of their beers, Anti-Hero IPA, has an image of a hop-headed military officer standing before a unit of hop soldiers parachuting out of the sky, presumably to do battle with your tongue. The beer itself is rich, deep, and refreshing with a solid malt backbone that holds up just enough to keep the hugely delicious pine and citrus hop attack from pummeling you to the floor. It's an IPA with an attitude, and it's the way all hop soldiers should be trained.

Illinois as a state is enjoying a renaissance of good food and drink. Chicago has more Michelin-starred restaurants than any other city in the country. It seems that every time you turn around another fantastic new local distillery has opened and is putting out great whiskey or gin. The local beer is on the cutting edge of the craft beer movement, and in the center of it all, Revolution is making a name for itself by delivering standout brews and servicing the community that both surrounds and energizes it.

Revolution Brewing offers six year-round beers: Anti-Hero IPA (6.5% ABV, 70 IBU), Eugene Porter (6.8% ABV, 28 IBU), Bottom Up Wit (5.0% ABV, 14 IBU), Coup D'Etat (French-style saison, 7.6% ABV, 50 IBU), Double Fist (double pale ale, 8.0% ABV, 90 IBU), and Cross of Gold (golden ale, 5.0% ABV, 25 IBU).

They also have eight special releases and six beers in their Hero series: Oktoberfest (5.7% ABV, 25 IBU), A Little Crazy (Belgian-style pale ale, 6.8% ABV), Rosa Hibiscus Ale (5.8% ABV, 15 IBU), Fistmas Ale (holiday ale, 6.1% ABV, 31 IBU), Mad Cow (milk stout, 7.7% ABV, 30 IBU), T.V. Party (rye IPA, 7.6% ABV, 80 IBU), Red Skull (imperial red ale, 8.3% ABV, 80 IBU), Unsessionable (imperial IPA, 10.0% ABV, 100 IBU), Galaxy Hero (IPA, 6.6% ABV, 80 IBU), Crystal Hero (IPA, 7.2% ABV, 80 IBU), Local Hero (IPA, 6.5% ABV, 65 IBU), Jukebox Hero (black IPA, 7.5% ABV, 75 IBU), Mosaic-Hero (IPA, 7.5% ABV, 65 IBU), and Citra Hero (IPA, 7.5% ABV, 85 IBU).

In addition, they have seven beers in their Deep Wood series, their barrel-aged beers: Very Mad Cow (barrel-aged milk stout, 9.7% ABV, 30 IBU), Straight Jacket (barrel-aged barleywine, 13.0% ABV, 55 IBU), Mean Gene (barrel-aged porter, 8.5% ABV), Bean Gene (barrel-aged porter with coffee, 9.0% ABV, 28 IBU), Blue Gene (barrel-aged porter with blueberry, 9.0% ABV, 28 IBU), Gravedigger Billy (barrel-aged Scotch ale, 10.4% ABV), and Deth's Tar (barrel-aged Russian imperial stout, 11.4% ABV, 40 IBU).

AROUND THE STATE

Goose Island Beer Company, Chicago

Goose Island Beer Company was started in 1988, after John Hall, the brewery's founder, had returned home from a trip to Europe. He had traveled across the Old World, sampling the wide styles and flavors of beers available there, and was determined to bring the experience home to America. His initial efforts were a success, and the brewery's reach began to grow. Then, in 1992, Goose Island etched its name forever in the craft brewing landscape by adding something new to the mix—bourbon barrel–aged beer. They were the pioneers of the process, subjecting the barreled beer to the wide fluctuations in heat and cold that are so characteristic of the Chicagoland area. The shift in temperature forces the liquid in and back out of the pores of the wood, imparting the sweet flavor of the whiskey still in the staves of the barrel into the beer. By 1995, Goose Island had become so popular that they had to open a larger brewery and a bottling plant, just to keep up with the demand. Lucky for us.

Half Acre Beer Company, Chicago

The Half Acre story, as the company's owners put it, "begins with boat loads of optimism" and is "full of piss and vinegar." Fortunately, their beer begins with boatloads of flavor and is full of hops and awesome. The brewery came into being in 2006 as a one-man show, set up in a spare bedroom. Its first beer was Half Acre Lager,

created with the help of a contract brewer in Wisconsin. It was brewed in a twenty-barrel brewhouse, fermented in forty-barrel tanks, packaged in 12-ounce bottles, and sold by a team of one in the nation's third-largest city, Chicago. The operation grew over time, and Half Acre eventually became the first brewery in Chicago to can its beers. They offer six year-round brews and more than twenty seasonals and special releases. If you've never tried their beer, start with a 16-ounce can of Daisy Cutter Pale Ale (5.2% ABV). It'll make you pucker with delight, and you can drink it all night long without falling over.

Illinois

➡ State capital: Springfield

➡ Illinois was the first state in the Union to ratify the Thirteenth Amendment, which abolished slavery, in 1865.

➡ Though there are conflicting reports of the invention of the ice cream "sundae," the city of Evanston, just north of Chicago, has a very legitimate claim to its creation. Because of pressure from the religious community, who believed the local soda fountains were corrupting the town's youth, the city banned the sale of ice cream sodas on the Sabbath. So, on Sundays, the "soda jerks," as they were called, began serving ice cream with syrup, leaving out the soda in order to comply with the law.

➡ The state ranks eleventh in the country for number of craft breweries, with a total of eighty-three.

➡ There are 9.3 million people of legal drinking age in the state, the average one of whom consumes 29.1 gallons of beer annually.

INDIANA

Three Floyds Brewing Company, Munster

ORIGIN

Three Floyds Brewing was founded, as you might guess, by three men all named Floyd. I know what you're thinking—Hi, my name is Floyd; this is my brother Floyd; and this is my other brother Floyd—and you are not that far off. In truth, the founders are brothers Nick and Simon, and their father Mike Floyd. In 1996, this beer-loving family opened their brewing operation in Hammond, Indiana. They started with just a few hundred dollars, a five-barrel, wok-burner-fired brew kettle (you know, those open-topped black metal contraptions that look like jet engines and are sometimes used by brave Thanksgiving Day chefs to deep-fry an entire turkey), and a handful of secondhand equipment. They moved the brewery to Munster in 2000 and opened a brewpub just next door in 2005.

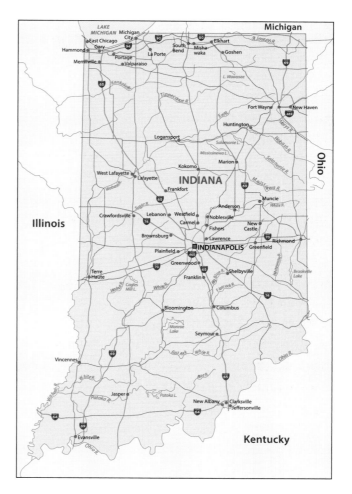

WHY THEY ROCK

No matter what's on tap or coming out of the barrels, the Floyd boys just make great beer. They are constantly trying new things, mixing up flavors and aging beers until they've created something new to bring to the brew-loving masses. Their beers are big, bold, luscious, and viscous, but never pretentious. What more can you ask from your beer?

Three Floyds offers eleven year-round brews: Yum Yum (American session ale, 5.5% ABV), Space Station Middle Finger (American pale ale, 6.0% ABV, 50 IBU), Backmasking (oatmeal stout, 5.9% ABV, 32 IBU), Permanent Funeral (pale ale, 10.5% ABV, 100 IBU), Alpha King (American pale ale, 6.6% ABV, 68 IBU), Robert the Bruce (Scottish-style ale, 6.5% ABV, 24 IBU), Gumballhead (wheat ale, 5.6% ABV, 35 IBU), Dreadnaught (imperial India pale ale, 9.5% ABV, 100 IBU), Zombie Dust (pale ale, 6.2% ABV, 50 IBU), Arctic Panzer Wolf (imperial pale ale, 9.0% ABV, 100 IBU), and Jinx Proof (pilsner, 5.1% ABV, 35 IBU).

In addition, they put out a huge number of barrel-aged brews: Tiberian Inquisitor (oak-aged Belgian-style ale, 9.5% ABV, 20 IBU), Spazzerack! (bourbon barrel–aged ale with star anise and orange, 9.0% ABV, 40 IBU), Ronaldo (port barrel–aged milk stout with cherries, 10.0% ABV), OWD English Barrel-Aged Barley Wine (12.2% ABV, 60 IBU), Murda'd Out Stout (13.9% ABV), Cuvee de Viking (barrel-aged rye wine, 10.0% ABV), Conquistador de la Muerte (barrel-aged milk stout, 10.0% ABV), Cabrito (barrel-aged Scottish-style ale, 9.5% ABV, 30 IBU), Cabra (whiskey barrel–aged Scottish-style ale with berries, 7.0% ABV, 30 IBU), Bully Guppy (cognac barrel–aged wheat beer with peaches, 5.6% ABV, 35 IBU), Bourbon Barrel–Aged Robert the Bruce with Raspberries (Scottish-style ale, 9.5% ABV, 30 IBU), Battle Priest (100 percent *Brett* fermented pinot noir barrel–aged wild ale), Barrel-Aged Moloko (milk stout, 10.0% ABV), Barrel-Aged Ice Grille (Belgian-style dubbel, 10.0% ABV, 18 IBU), Barrel-Aged Dark Lord de Muerte (Russian imperial stout with ancho and guajillo peppers, 15.0% ABV), Barrel-Aged Black Sun Stout (8.5% ABV, 50 IBU).

They also release eleven seasonals, a whopping thirty-two collaborations with other brewers, and more than fifty brewpub exclusives. Obviously, not all of these beers are constantly available. You know what they say: You can drink all of the beers some of the time, and you can drink some of the beers all of the time, but you can't drink all of the beers all of the time. That was Abraham Lincoln, right? I'm sure that's how it went.

AROUND THE STATE

Upland Brewing Company, Bloomington

If Upland Brewing Company is to be believed, the origins of their brewery date back to the last ice age. That is, they give the credit for their heritage to a glacier—the one that wore down and carved out the flat plains of the American Midwest, stopping just short of the southern part of Indiana, which is now known as the Uplands. According to the brewery, the unique land formation caused by this glacier attracted a particular type of settler: those who were connected to the land, looked out for their community, and cared very deeply for their craftsmanship. Though the brewery didn't actually open for business until 1998, it's this deep heritage, of the community that came before, that forms the philosophical backbone of Upland Brewing Company and makes them care so very much about crafting great beer.

People's Brewing Company, Lafayette

The city of Lafayette, Indiana, has a long history of brewing. There were no fewer than six operating breweries in the city before that darkest of dark periods known as Prohibition. Of those, only the Lafayette Brewing Company lived through that horrific era and still brews on today. The People's Brewing Company aims to continue the rich tradition that has been a part of the city since 1855. They brew in a 6,000-square-foot facility (which includes a 1,000-square-foot taproom) and distribute their beer in pints, growlers, cans, and bottles. They have twelve taps, two of which are on nitrogen, offering a regular rotation of craft-brewed, small-batch beer. Among those you may find on those taps when you visit are Moundbuilder IPA (6.5% ABV, 88 IBU), Aberrant Amber (5.5% ABV, 48 IBU), Farmer's Daughter Wheat (4.2% ABV, 17 IBU), People's Pilsner (4.5% ABV, 42 IBU), Mr. Brown (American-style brown ale, 7.0% ABV, 47 IBU), Sgt. Bravo Pale Ale (4.8% ABV, 39 IBU), Nine Irish Ale (Irish red ale, 4.3% ABV, 17 IBU), Notorious B.I.P. (American-style black IPA, 6.5% ABV, 75 IBU), Procrastinator Helles Bock (American-style amber, 7.2% ABV, 36 IBU), Space Cowboy IPA (9.0% ABV, 96 IBU), and Rail Jumper Stout (4.5% ABV, 42 IBU).

Indiana

➡ State capital: Indianapolis

➡ Indianapolis is the site of one of the largest game conventions in the world—Gen Con—which features all the dice, cards, board games, miniatures, role-playing games, and accoutrements that anyone could need. Good stuff to occupy your time while you sip a delicious brew.

➡ In 1904, there were forty-one breweries in the state of Indiana. By 1914, that number had dropped to thirty-one, but the number of brewery employees increased during that period, rising to a total of 2,207. All legitimate breweries in the state, however, were shut down by 1918 due to Prohibition.

➡ There was actually an Indiana state prohibition law in the 1850s, due to the same temperance movement that eventually caused the national "Time of Great Suffering." The state law, however, was eventually shot down by the Indiana Supreme Court.

➡ There are 4.6 million persons of legal drinking age in the state, the average one of whom consumes 25.9 gallons of beer annually.

IOWA

Toppling Goliath Brewing Company, Decorah

ORIGIN

The batches are small, but the taste is gigantic. Isn't that a lovely phrase? It's perhaps the best way to describe the beer made by Toppling Goliath Brewing Company. Started in 2009 in Decorah, Iowa, with a modest half-barrel brewery and taproom, they call themselves a stealth brewery, flying under the radar, and this is true. Decorah, Iowa, is, well, a long way from any major metropolitan center. Toppling Goliath doesn't have a long list of medals from prestigious brewing competitions; they only distribute their beers in Iowa and Wisconsin, and only a few of their beers are bottled. But that should just go to reinforce how truly fantastic their beers are when you consider that their Pseudo Sue APA has been ranked the number two beer *in the world* by BeerAdvocate.com and RateBeer.com. They have three other beers that have been rated in the top five on both sites.

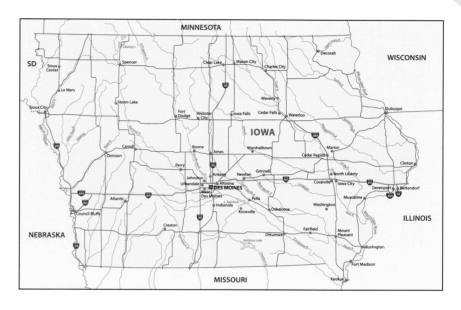

WHY WE LOVE THEM

One of the key philosophies that guides Toppling Goliath is that they try to bottle, label, and sell their beer all within a twenty-four-hour window, so that the beer reaches the consumer in the freshest possible state. The only way to get it fresher is to go to their taproom, which is open Sunday to Tuesday from noon to 8 p.m.; Wednesday and Thursday from noon to 9 p.m.; Friday and Saturday from noon to 10 p.m.; and will require some driving. Prepare to stay the night.

You know what they say: If it was easy to get, everybody would drink it. That's very true. Toppling Goliath takes us back to the days when craft brewing first started to reignite the imagination of beer drinkers all over this nation. The small batches make it rare and hard to come by. The effort required to obtain some makes it desirable. The brewery's stealth nature means that word of their existence is spread only from devotee to devotee, and knowing their name and location somehow makes you part of the club. The superb crafting of their beers makes you realize just what a prize you hold in your hands, and getting a taste of their wares feels like a real discovery—just like it did the first time

you opened a craft beer and realized you were on to something. That day you felt like you had opened the door to a new world, a place that not many people had yet discovered. Toppling Goliath has recreated for us the perfect storm of discoverable aspects. They've given us back the wonder and the desire to seek that which is so hard to obtain. That feeling of adventure and discovery—as well as their damn good beer—is why they are among the best in the nation.

Toppling Goliath offers fourteen regular and seasonal brews: Dorothy's New World Lager (5.5% ABV, 11 IBU), Golden Nugget IPA (6.0% ABV, 56 IBU), Tsunami Pale Ale (5.0% ABV, 31 IBU), Tsunami Dark Ale (amber ale, 5.5% ABV, 60 IBU), Psuedo Sue (pale ale, 5.8% ABV, 50 IBU), Murph's Irish Red (5.0% ABV), Rover Truck Oatmeal Stout (5.7% ABV, 35 IBU), Naughty 90 Oaked IPA (6.2% ABV, 100+ IBU), Rush Pilsner (4.7% ABV), Rush Hollow Maple Ale (farmhouse ale, 7.0% ABV, 16 IBU), Light Speed Pale Ale (5.8% ABV), Robusto Porter (5.8% ABV), Tsunami Surf (pale ale, 5.5% ABV), and Smoove Opferator (brown ale, 5.5% ABV).

They also offer a fantastic series, known as the Hop Patrol. These beers are "aggressively" hopped to "save your palate from boring beer!" Each brew is crafted to bring out the qualities of a single individual hop variety or a distinct blending of hops. The patrol members are ZeeLander IPA (5.5% ABV, 80 IBU), Biter IPA (6.6% ABV, 88 IBU), Hopsmack Double IPA (8.0% ABV, 175 IBU!), 1492 IPA (6.0% ABV, 45 IBU), Twisted Galaxy Double IPA (7.2% ABV, 170 IBU!), Alternate Galaxy IPA (6.6% ABV, 98 IBU), Intergalactic Warrior IPA (5.8% ABV, 60 IBU), Pompeii IPA (5.5% ABV, 60 IBU), and Sosus Double IPA (8.0% ABV, 100+ IBU).

AROUND THE STATE

■ Peace Tree Brewing Company, Knoxville

The name of the brewery is taken from a historic sycamore tree that resided near the town of Red Rock. Though the area where it lived is now under Lake Red Rock, the Peace Tree was estimated to be the second-largest tree of its kind. The shade of its branches was reputedly a spot where generations of Native Americans met to talk, trade, and deal with tribal business. In the late sixties, the Red Rock Dam was built to create a reservoir for the Des Moines River, lowering the water level in the lake. The Peace Tree, now over 500 years old, was still standing and can be seen today, its huge, weathered-away trunk lifting out of the waters. Though Peace Tree Brewing was only started in 2009 and has a long while before it catches up with the age of its namesake, the brewery aims to be a uniting force for the beer-loving community in Iowa, just as the Peace Tree was for people in its time.

■ 515 Brewing Company, Clive

515 Brewing Company has an unusual origin story. It all started as a secret plot. Apparently, two of the founders' wives hatched a scheme that would enable them to spend more time together. They convinced their husbands, Ryan and Brandon, to brew beer together—knowing that if their husbands were occupied for the day making beer, that would leave the wives free to do whatever they pleased. Little did they know—several years later, and with the addition of two more brewers—that their little plan would end up making beer history. Thank heaven for small favors.

Iowa

➡ State capital: Des Moines

➡ It used to be that beers brewed in Iowa were not allowed to exceed 6.0% ABV. This put Iowa brewers at a disadvantage, since out-of-state brewers were not subject to this same restriction and could freely distribute brews of higher alcohol content. However, in 2010 this restriction was lifted, allowing brewers to craft beers up to 12% ABV. Since that time, the number of breweries in the state has doubled.

➡ Iowa ranks in thirtieth place among all states in total population, weighing in at 3.1 million.

➡ Iowa is bounded by the Mississippi River on the east and the Missouri River on the west. It has ninety-nine counties, 100 county seats, and is home to the largest Amish community west of the Mississippi River.

➡ There are 2.2 million persons of legal drinking age in the state, the average one of whom consumes 33.6 gallons of beer annually.

KANSAS

Walnut River Brewing Company, El Dorado

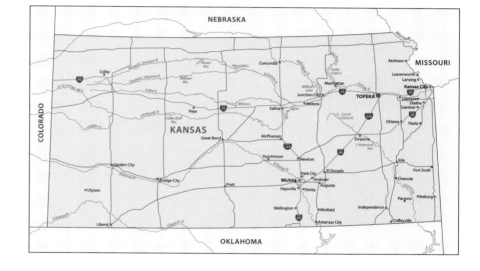

⭐ ORIGIN

The building Walnut River Brewing Company calls home has had an interesting life. In truth, it's lived several lives. Built somewhere between 1917 and 1920, the red brick building has housed a general supply store, a grocery store, a creamery, a bakery, two different storage companies, and a plastics company. It was even a brothel back in 1923, during that darkest of dark stains in the grand tapestry of American history—Prohibition.

It was called Goldie's Place back then. The brothel occupied the upper floor of the two-story building; it resided upstairs from first a supply company, then a grocery store, and then a creamery. It lasted in that spot for more than twenty years until a baker purchased the entire building. Then Goldie and her girls had to move out.

Today, of course, that red brick building is home to Walnut River Brewing. The two founders, Rick Goehring and B.J. Hunt, are what you might call the dynamic duo of beer in Kansas. Rick is the head brewer. In addition to having been a home brewer before going pro, Rick took the time to go through the American Brewers Guild Craftbrewers

Apprenticeship Program, an intensive six months geared toward learning all the ins and outs of running a craft brewery. B.J., on the other hand, is a serial entrepreneur. Having started and run businesses his whole life, B.J. brings the other half of the brewery business equation—the parts under the hood, like dealing with regulatory agencies and bringing the product to market, that make the whole operation hum. Together Rick and B.J. have built a cool place for their friends, neighbors, and other residents of El Dorado, Kansas, to come grab a cold one and relax after a long day.

WHY THEY ARE SO DAMN COOL

Kansas has a deep history with beer. The territory that became the thirty-fourth state was added to the United States as part of the Louisiana Purchase in 1803. The Kansas-Nebraska Act of 1854 opened up the territory to further settlement, and many of those who came to the new frontier had immigrated from Germany. They, of course, brought with them their love of beer. The first farmers who attempted to make a living in the area tried to grow corn and raise pigs. But the climate proved to be inhospitable for those endeavors, so they were forced to change to growing wheat.

That wheat now forms part of the backbone for many of the delicious brews made at Walnut River Brewing.

Other than hefeweizen and a few specialty brews, most beers consist of an all-barley mash bill. Adding a bit of wheat to, say, an IPA recipe, adds a nice soft roundness to the sweet body of the beer. It provides a subtle backdrop that allows the brewer's chosen hops to really take center stage. The wheat smooths out any rough edges, making the beer more approachable, easier to drink, and more suitable to be enjoyed with a wide variety of cuisines.

The folks at Walnut River Brewing infuse a little bit of Kansas into all of their beers. They take the best the state has to offer and turn it into liquid gold. It's this dedication and passion to delivering a most excellent pint that earns them top honors.

Walnut River Brewing offers up five delicious brews: Falconer's Wheat (a hopped-up wheat beer made with Falconer's Flight hops that weighs in at 5.3% ABV and 21.7 IBU); Coffee Porter (a robust porter brewed with a secret recipe that comes out at 6.3% ABV and 37.5 IBU); High Beam IPA (an American-style IPA that features a little bit of wheat to balance out two different roasts of caramel malt and Falconer's Flight hops; it comes in at a hefty 7.7% ABV and 64.8 IBU); Warbeard Irish Red (an Irish red ale brewed with a touch of chocolate malt and some punch-you-in-the-face Magnum hops that weighs in at 5.5% ABV and 23.3 IBU); and Teter Rock Kölsch (an easy-drinking Kölsch-style beer that boasts a modest 4.7% ABV and 26.3 IBU).

AROUND THE STATE

Free State Brewing Company, Lawrence

The Free State Brewing Company opened its doors in 1989, making it the first legal brewery in the state of Kansas in more than 100 years. Today, the company has a fourteen-barrel brewhouse and distributes its brews to beer lovers all over Kansas, Nebraska, and Missouri. The brewers' flagship beers include Ad Astra Ale (amber ale, 31 IBU), Yakimaniac IPA (68 IBU), Oatmeal Stout (42 IBU), and Copperhead Pale Ale (53 IBU). In addition, they offer seasonal brews: Octoberfest (fall release, 25 IBU), Brinkley's Maibock (spring release, 14 IBU), and Stormchaser IPA (summer release, 59 IBU).

River City Brewing Company, Wichita

River City Brewing has been around a while, having opened their brewery in 1993. They are the first brewpub in Wichita and only the third brewery to open in Kansas in more than fifty years. River City Brewing offers sixteen different beers on tap, including seasonal and rotational brews. No matter what has been tapped, you will always find these five daily pours available: Rock Island Red (6.0% ABV), Emerald City Stout (5.7% ABV), Old Town Brown Ale (5.5% ABV), Tornado Alley IPA (7.0% ABV), and Harvester Wheat Ale (5.0% ABV).

Kansas

➡ State capital: Topeka

➡ The name *Kansas* came from the Sioux word meaning "people of the south wind."

➡ The state has some of the strictest alcohol laws in the nation and has for more than 100 years. Statewide prohibition started in 1881, thirty-nine years before the Eighteenth Amendment took effect. Prohibition in Kansas lasted until 1948, fifteen years after the Twenty-First Amendment repealed Prohibition nationwide.

➡ Kansas ranks thirty-fourth among the states for number of craft breweries, with a total of fifty-nine.

➡ There are 2 million persons of legal drinking age in the state, the average one of whom consumes 28.3 gallons of beer annually.

KENTUCKY

Against the Grain Brewery & Smokehouse, Louisville

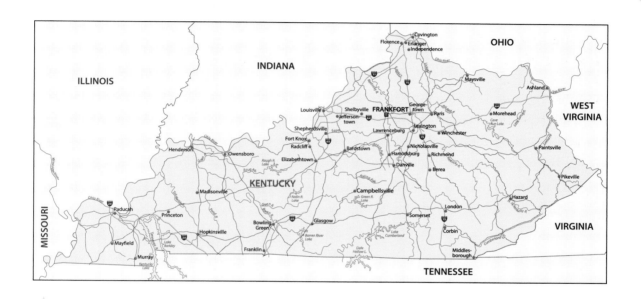

⭐ ORIGIN

Against the Grain Brewery & Smokehouse held its grand opening on October 4, 2011. Their facility is inside a former train station and houses one of the nation's only operational, Victorian-style "showpiece" brewhouses—a three-story, copper-clad, fifteen-barrel work of art. It is Louisville's only brewer-owned brewpub.

If you are a baseball fan, like me, you will be excited to learn that Against the Grain is situated just across the street from Louisville Slugger Field. The stadium is the home of the Louisville Bats (appropriate, considering the namesake of their home field), which is the AAA affiliate team of the Cincinnati Reds.

WHY THEY ARE AMONG THE BEST

Against the Grain has a sincerely impressive list of beers in their collection. These are beers that are either regularly brewed, sometimes brewed, rarely brewed, or have at one time been brewed at their facility. They keep track of the list on their web page, and at last glance the beers numbered over 140. The names are frequently puns: Citra Wet Ass Down, Dirty Hoppin' ScondrAle, Judas Yeast, Rauncho Man Randy Beverage, Pepperation H, Ryern Maiden, We Shuck on the First Date, We Spelt It Wrong, Sam & Adams Bossin Lager...the list goes on and on and on. It's worth dropping by their site just to read the names. Looking them over is like listening to that hilarious friend you had in college who could sit in the corner and make bad jokes all night long without even cracking a smile. My Hammy Weiss! Mockless Lobster!

As you can imagine, at a brewery named Against the Grain, the owners don't do things the same way other breweries do. They don't have a standard set of flagship beers that they put out on a regular basis. Instead, they "brew a spectrum of beers" within six categories that they have defined: Hop, Smoke, Dark, Malt, Session, and Whim. They claim that if you have an affinity for any one of those flavors/types on any given night, they will be able to satisfy your craving. Hop, Smoke, Dark, Malt, and Session are easy to wrap your brain around. But Whim? You might say that Whim is what Against the Grain is all about.

Instead of being pinned down by a set of industry standards or ideals of what a brewery should produce, the fellows at Against the Grain let creativity rule the day. In essence, they create a specialty beer in each of their six categories every time they brew. In the case of Whim, they let their imaginations run wild. This is where the monsters are unleashed. This is where the demons that live in the deep recesses of the mind live and where the evil masterminds at the brewery can let those caged libidinal freaks finally run free. Whim is like the chef's tasting menu at a fancy restaurant, or the manager's selection at your local steakhouse. It's the Omakase at that great sushi restaurant down the street or the grab bag at the candy store when you were a kid. Whim is all of these things put together with the evil twist of a mustache and a cackle thrown in for good measure. Whim is what craft beer should be about. Need I say more?

AROUND THE STATE

Bluegrass Brewing Company, Louisville

Bluegrass Brewing Company started in 1993 when Pat Hagan, recently graduated from an intensive brewing course at Siebel Institute in Chicago, returned home to Kentucky and convinced his father to partner with him to open a brewpub. Louisville was, in the Hagans' estimation, in desperate need of some good hoppy beer and a great place to enjoy said beer. And so, the BBC Brewpub in St. Mathews was born. In 2002, the father-son pair bought the Pipkin Brewing Company and started offering their delicious beers in both kegs and bottles. As a result, their brand has grown year after year, and their beer has spread to the beerly devoted in Kentucky, Indiana, Ohio, Tennessee, and Virginia. In 2006, they opened a second Bluegrass Brewing Company brewpub, and in 2010 a third, where they offer five year-round beers on tap and five seasonally available brews.

Alltech Lexington Brewing and Distilling Company, Lexington

Alltech Lexington Brewing and Distilling is a member of a very exclusive group: "brewstilleries," operations that both brew beer and distill spirits. Being from Kentucky, the heartland of some of America's best whiskeys, it makes perfect sense. It drifts over into the "genius" realm when you consider that they use their ex-bourbon barrels to age their Kentucky Bourbon Barrel Ale and Kentucky Bourbon Barrel Stout. The brewery was founded by Dr. Pearse Lyons, an Irish entrepreneur who interned at both the Guinness and Harp breweries while he was just a young lad. Dr. Lyons went on to become the first Irishman to get a formal degree in brewing and distilling from the British School of Malting and Brewing, and eventually brought the world some of the best beer from Kentucky.

Kentucky

➡ State capital: Frankfort

➡ The name *Kentucky* comes from an Iroquois word meaning "land of tomorrow."

➡ The song "Happy Birthday to You" is reputed to have been created by two sisters from Louisville, Kentucky, in 1893.

➡ Kentucky was the fifteenth state to join the Union and was the first on the western frontier.

➡ Surprisingly, given the fact that Kentucky is the epicenter of bourbon production in America, the laws governing alcohol in the state are some of the most confusing in the nation. The state issues more than seventy different types of alcohol licenses and divides itself into three different types of counties: dry (no alcohol sales), wet (full retail sales of alcohol), and moist (which is sort of a middle ground between dry and wet).

➡ There are 3.2 million persons of legal drinking age in the state, the average one of whom consumes 24.4 gallons of beer annually.

LOUISIANA

NOLA Brewing, New Orleans

⭐ ORIGIN

NOLA Brewing, or if you are being formal, the New Orleans Lager & Ale Brewing Company, started putting out craft beer in 2009. It was the first commercial brewery to operate in New Orleans after Hurricane Katrina devastated the city. The last brewery to operate in the city had been run by the Dixie Brewing Company, which had started operations in 1907. But when the city had been de-watered and it was safe to return, the brewery was found in an inoperable state and was officially shut down in 2005.

The return of craft brewing to the New Orleans area actually began in 2006, when founder Kirk Coco got out of the navy and returned to his home to begin brewing beer. He knew what he wanted to do when he returned home. The trouble was, he didn't know how to do it—he didn't know how to brew beer. But problems of this sort rarely slow down

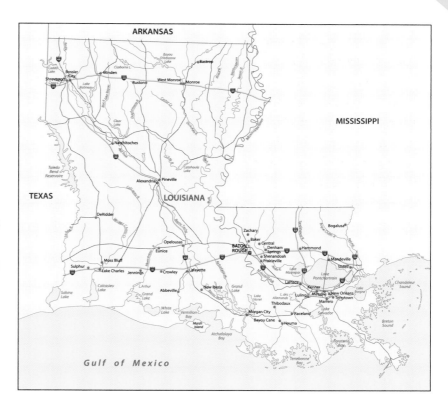

or even a single piece of brewing equipment, Kirk sat down with his prospective brewmaster over a pint of beer and gave him the sales pitch. Less than a year removed from seeing the brewery he had worked at for almost twenty years destroyed by a hurricane, and in a city that was still not fully recovered from the devastation, Peter's desire for stability was probably overwhelming. Despite all that, he took the risk, accepted the position at the not-yet-a-brewery, and NOLA became a reality.

WHY THEY DESERVE THE LOVE

NOLA is the first brewery to make a cask-conditioned beer in the city of New Orleans since the "thirteen years of doom" (also known as Prohibition). Unlike their year-round and seasonal releases, these beers are more experimental, using fresh fruit and spices to create brand-new flavors and explore new territory. If you are lucky enough to be in New Orleans when one of these casks is opened, you will be treated with a host of new beer additives, including pineapple, papaya, plum, honey, peach, poblano pepper, and honey.

It's their dedication to their community and to their craft that makes NOLA's

an intrepid entrepreneur, and such was the case with Kirk. Setting out to find a brewmaster, he discovered that the man he needed to get was Peter Caddoo. Peter had been at Dixie Brewing Company for nearly two full decades, and now that his former employer was closed, Mr. Caddoo was looking for new opportunities in a city that was slowly pulling itself out of the water.

The trouble was, by the time Kirk had located Peter, the brewmaster had already accepted a job at a chain brewpub. Again, the entrepreneur went into problem-solving mode. Though he didn't yet have a brewery brewers rise to such heights. They are undaunted explorers, returning to ground that has seen its fair share of difficulties, but turning that difficulty into an opportunity. The spirit of Louisiana is strong, especially in New Orleans. It's a unique part of the country. This determination to cling to a heritage and a past that is proud and cannot be drowned out, even by natural disasters, is at the heart of the Creole culture and is a major driving force behind NOLA Brewing.

The New Orleans Lager & Ale Brewing Company puts out five year-round brews and three seasonals (subject to change each year): NOLA Blonde (4.9% ABV), NOLA Brown (3.9% ABV), Hopitoulas (6.0% ABV), 7th Street Wheat (4.5% ABV), Irish Channel Stout (6.8% ABV), Hurricane Saison (summer seasonal, 6.5% ABV), Flambeau Red (spring seasonal, 5.7% ABV), and Smoky Mary (fall seasonal, 5.3% ABV).

AROUND THE STATE

Bayou Teche, Arnaudville

Bayou Teche was created with a sole purpose in mind—to make beer that would complement the spicy Cajun kick that is the hallmark of the food from Louisiana. The decision to start the brewery occurred on St. Patrick's Day 2009. The founders, the Knott brothers—Karlos, Byron, and Dorsey—cleaned up an old railroad car and turned it into one of the best breweries in the country. They offer five year-round beers: LA 31 Bière Pâle (pale ale, 5.7% ABV, 27 IBU), LA 31 Boucanée (smoked wheat ale, 6.0% ABV, 14 IBU), LA 31 Bière Noire (black ale, 5.25% ABV, 19 IBU), LA 31 Passionne (passion fruit wheat ale, 5.5% ABV, 12 IBU), and Acadie (bière de garde, 6.0% ABV, 21 IBU). They also put out three seasonal beers: Courir de Mardi Gras (bière de mars, available during Mardi Gras, 6.2% ABV, 15 IBU), Saison D'Ecrevisses (saison, available January to June, 6.0% ABV, 21 IBU), and Cocodrie (Belgian-style IPA, available July to December, 8.0% ABV, 60 IBU).

Abita Brewing Company, Abita Springs

The Abita Brewing Company was founded in 1986, just thirty miles north of New Orleans. That year, the owners brewed 1,500 barrels of beer. The response from the thirsty masses was overwhelmingly positive, and before long they had outgrown the capacity of their space and found themselves in need of a move. And so, in 1994, they did just that, taking their brewing operations just up the road, staying in Abita Springs and transforming their original space into a 100-seat brewpub. Though they now brew in much larger quantities (151,000 barrels of beer a year and an additional 9,100 barrels of root beer), they still brew everything in small batches, adhering to the recipe for success that has made them a beer drinker's favorite nationwide.

Louisiana

➡ State capital: Baton Rouge

➡ Louisiana was originally named in honor of King Louis XIV of France, and has the tallest state capitol building in the Union, with thirty-four floors rising to a grand total of 450 feet.

➡ It is considered a simple assault if, while in Louisiana, you bite someone with your natural teeth. If you try to do that with your false teeth, though, it is considered aggravated assault, and you can get a steeper sentence.

➡ As a rule of thumb, the colder the state, the more beer it consumes per capita. Louisiana, however, bucks that trend. There are 3.3 million persons of legal drinking age in Louisiana, the average one of whom consumes 33.9 gallons of beer annually.

MAINE

Allagash Brewing Company, Portland

⭐ ORIGIN

Allagash Brewing Company started in 1995, during the very early years of the craft brew movement in the United States. Back then it was a one-man show: just Rob Tod, his brew kettle, and a desire to make great beer. Rob realized that while beer was beginning to have a renaissance across the country, the styles that were represented were primarily English and German. Having done a fair amount of travel, Rob himself had cultivated an affinity for Belgian-style beers, a style that was underrepresented in the marketplace.

So the intrepid beerman set up shop and began to remedy that problem. He started by designing and building a fifteen-barrel brewhouse and filling it with the ingredients he would need to create great beer. His first product was Allagash White, a Belgian-style "wit" beer that uses wheat in place of barley

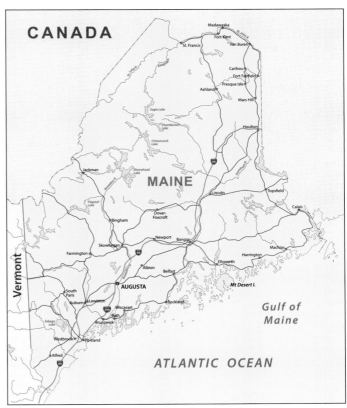

and balances the flavor with orange peel and spices, rather than hops. He brewed this beer with his own proprietary strain of yeast, and in the summer of 1995, he released it to the world.

Its success was immediate, and the brewery began to grow, offering more beers and hiring people to help. In 2001, the brewery refined the process, pushing its Belgian-influenced beers further toward mastery. In that year, the company discontinued the bottle cap, preferring instead a cork stopper and holding it in place with a wire cage. This was the way the monks bottled their beers, and so it would be the way Allagash would do it as well. In addition, the brewers moved to bottle conditioning their beers, adding sugar to the residual yeast in the bottled beer, creating natural carbonation and also allowing the yeast to consume the excess oxygen trapped inside after the cork was put on—just as the monks had.

Today Allagash brewers offer seven year-round brews, four specialty beers, and a very long list of unique releases. They stick very closely to the Belgian brewing traditions that brought success in the past and have made them one of the most distinguished brewers in America.

WHY WE CALL THEM GURU

When you look over the list of beers Allagash puts out, you can't help but be impressed with the dedication the brewers have put into following their passion. Belgian-style beers are what they set out to bring to the United States—American-made Belgian-style beers, not Belgian imports. They have done this, consistently, while educating an entire generation of beer drinkers about a whole new style of brew, effectively injecting a completely new dimension into the craft brew landscape. They are among the leaders of the craft brew movement, visionaries who opened new horizons for the thirsty masses. They have honed their craft, not only staying true to its traditions, but also pushing into new territory, taking Belgian-style beers and making them their own. They have been a stalwart guide on our journey into the realm of great beer. For that, they deserve our thanks and our praise.

The Allagash year-round brews are as follows: Allagash White (Belgian-style wheat, 5.0% ABV), Allagash Dubbel (Belgian-style dubbel, 7.0% ABV), Allagash Tripel (strong golden ale, 9.0% ABV), Allagash Black (Belgian-style stout, 7.5% ABV), Allagash Curieux (bourbon barrel–aged strong ale, 11.0% ABV), Allagash House Beer (available only at the brewery, 4.5% ABV), and Allagash Saison (6.1% ABV).

Their specialty beers are Allagash Odyssey (oak-aged dark wheat, limited annual release, 10.4% ABV), Allagash Confluence Ale (dry-hopped golden ale, limited annual release, 7.5% ABV), Allagash Interlude (wine barrel–aged farmhouse ale, limited annual release, 9.5% ABV), and Allagash Grand Cru (spiced winter ale, limited yearly release, 7.2% ABV).

AROUND THE STATE

Shipyard Brewing Company, Portland

Shipyard Brewing Company got its start in the back room of a restaurant. In 1992, Federal Jack's Restaurant & Brew Pub opened in Kennebunkport Harbor. The operation was started by entrepreneur Fred Forsley and master brewer Alan Pugsley. Alan, an Englishman, had learned the craft of beer making at the Ringwood Brewery in Hampshire. Two years later, in 1994, the thirsty masses were consuming more of the brewery's beer than its founders could produce in the brewpub, and so the pair officially opened the Shipyard Brewing Company in Portland, Maine. Another two years and Shipyard had captured the distinction of being the fastest-growing craft brewery in America. Today it is one of the largest in the country, producing nearly 170,000 barrels of beer each year. The company puts out a combined twenty different English-style and seasonal beers, which are distributed in forty states and in a few select countries outside the United States.

Maine Beer Company, Freeport

The Maine Beer Company was started by two brothers—one a lawyer by trade, the other an instigator by nature. The two would spend their weekends together, brewing beer. By their own admission, they made some good beer and some bad

beer, but the point was that they enjoyed the time they spent together. Gradually their brewing became more sophisticated, their equipment more and more specialized. That's when the instigator turned to the lawyer and said, "What would you rather do with the rest of your life? Be a lawyer or a brewer?" And in that moment, the Maine Beer Company was conceived. They focused at first on perfecting just one recipe, making sure they could reach the standard of beer that they would be proud to drink and call their own. They did that and officially started brewing as a company in 2009. Today, they give 1 percent of their sales to environmental nonprofit organizations, and they make damn good beer.

Maine

➡ State capital: Augusta

➡ Maine weighs in at twentieth place among the fifty states in number of craft breweries, at forty-seven.

➡ Maine has 3,478 miles of coastline. That's more than California and enough to give the state the third-longest coast behind only Florida and Louisiana. In addition, there are enough deep harbors that all the ships in all the world's navies could safely anchor along that coast.

➡ There are 1 million persons of legal drinking age in Maine, the average one of whom consumes 34.0 gallons of beer annually.

MARYLAND

Flying Dog Brewery, Frederick

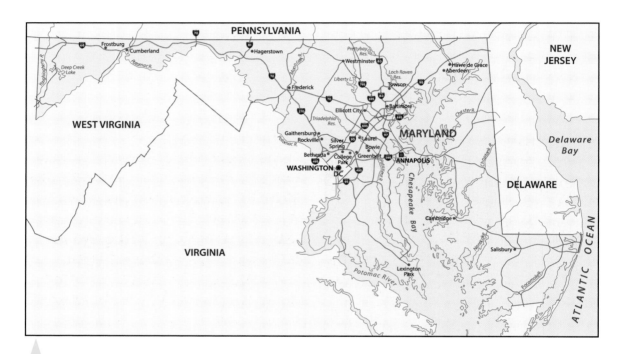

★ ORIGIN

The name Flying Dog, as you might imagine, has a very interesting story behind it. That story starts with a group of adventurers who had set out to climb K2, the world's second-highest peak. The mountain must have a chip on its shoulder for being only the second-highest on the planet, because for every four people who manage to reach the summit, one person has died trying. Among the adventurers who climbed the deadly mountain was George Stranahan, the eventual founder of the brewery. His group managed to not only climb K2, but all returned to tell the tale as well. However, one tragedy befell them on the climb—by day seventeen of their thirty-five-day trip, they had run out of alcohol.

Settling into their hotel when they got back, triumphant but exceptionally thirsty, the group managed to get themselves some alcohol. Sitting there with drink in hand, George spotted a painting on the wall. It was a huge oil painting of a dog. The dog had "left the ground." Somehow, the absurdity of their more-than-a-month-long adventure combined with the odd image of the "flying dog" sparked something in the group. So in 1990, George Stranahan created the Flying Dog Brewpub in Aspen, Colorado. The brewpub grew into a full-fledged brewery and eventually moved to Maryland, where it continues to put out great beer today.

WHY THEY ARE ONE OF THE BIG DOGS

Flying Dog has eleven year-round releases: Easy IPA (American session IPA, 4.7% ABV, 50 IBU), Bloodline Blood Orange Ale (7.0% ABV, 40 IBU), The Truth Imperial IPA (8.7% ABV, 120 IBU), Raging Bitch Belgian-Style IPA (8.3% ABV, 60 IBU), Snake Dog India Pale Ale (7.1% ABV, 60 IBU), Flying Dog Pale Ale (5.5% ABV, 35 IBU), Pearl Necklace Oyster Stout (5.5% ABV, 35 IBU), Flying Dog Hefeweizen (4.7% ABV, 12 IBU), Old Scratch Amber Lager (5.5% ABV, 19.5 IBU), Gonzo Imperial Porter (9.2% ABV, 85 IBU), and Double Dog Double IPA (11.5% ABV, 85 IBU).

They also put out ten seasonal brews: Dead Rise Old Bay Summer Ale (5.6% ABV, 25 IBU), Woody Creek Belgian White (4.8% ABV, 17 IBU), Dogtoberfest Marzen (5.6% ABV, 30 IBU), Secret Stash

Harvest Ale (5.5% ABV, 45 IBU), The Fear Imperial Pumpkin Ale (9.0% ABV, 45 IBU), K-9 Winter Ale (7.4% ABV, 30 IBU), Kujo Imperial Coffee Stout (8.9% ABV, 40 IBU), Horn Dog Barley Wine (10.2% ABV, 45 IBU), Lucky SOB Irish Red Ale (5.5% ABV, 28 IBU), and Barrel-Aged Gonzo Imperial Porter (9.2% ABV, 85 IBU).

Gonzo Imperial Porter is, of course, an homage to the "gonzo journalist" Hunter S. Thompson. As the story goes, Thompson lived just down the street from George's Flying Dog Ranch. They eventually became friends, bonding over their shared love of drinking and firearms. In 1990, Thompson introduced George to Ralph Steadman; who illustrated many of Thompson's works, and in 1995 the famous artist began creating labels for the brewery.

To sum up, then: Their labels are drawn by Ralph Steadman, the founder of the brewery climbed K2 and was friends with Hunter S. Thompson; and the company makes great beer. Could a brewery be any cooler?

AROUND THE STATE

■ DuClaw Brewing Company, Baltimore

Dave Benfield, the founder of the DuClaw Brewing Company, is a very honest man. How do I know this? Because when asked why he started home brewing in college, he will look you in the eye and tell you that he did it to "meet women." Sure, it's nice to have gallons and gallons of beer to drink after you've finished, but Dave is man enough to admit that he had an ulterior motive. Fortunately for us, he became hooked on the hobby, and in 1995 he went pro, opening the doors of the DuClaw Brewing Company of Bel Air in 1996. He offers a huge list of beers, many of which are available year-round, others of which are available only when the ingredients are fresh and inspiration to brew them arises. Among those that are always available on tap are Bare Ass Blonde Ale (5.0% ABV, 19 IBU), Euforia Toffee Nut Brown Ale (5.0% ABV, 22 IBU), Hellrazer IPA (7.5% ABV, 85 IBU), Misfit Red Amber Ale (5.1% ABV, 23 IBU), Serum XXIPA (9.0% ABV, 80 IBU), and Sweet Baby Jesus Chocolate Peanut Butter Porter (6.5% ABV, 53 IBU).

Evolution Craft Brewing Company, Salisbury

Evolution Craft Brewing was started in 2009 inside an old grocery store. The company's creators strive to bring about the "evolution" of craft beer, delivering to the thirsty masses new and interesting tastes in both regular and special release. They offer five year-round mainline beers: Exile Red Ale (5.9% ABV, 48 IBU), Lot No. 3 IPA (6.8% ABV, 65 IBU), Lucky 7 Porter (5.8% ABV, 24 IBU), Lot No. 6 Double IPA (8.5% ABV, 75 IBU), and Primal Pale Ale (5.0% ABV, 30 IBU). They also release four seasonal brews: Jacques Au Lantern (unfiltered amber ale, released August 1, 6.3% ABV, 20 IBU), Secret Spot Winter Ale (altbier, released November 1, 6.3% ABV, 40 IBU), Sprung (golden ale, released January 1, 4.9% ABV, 14 IBU), and Summer Session Ale (released April 1, 4.6% ABV, 25 IBU).

Maryland

➡ State capital: Annapolis

➡ The first umbrella factory in the United States was created in Baltimore, Maryland, in 1828, and the first post office system in the country was established there as well in 1774.

➡ During the Revolutionary period, Rockville was known as Hungerford's Tavern, which was the town's most famous landmark. It is said that the first calls to throw off the shackles of British rule were heard at this tavern in 1774.

➡ Maryland ranks twenty-fifth in the United States for number of craft breweries with thirty-four.

➡ There are 4.3 million persons of legal drinking age in the state, the average one of whom consumes 23.2 gallons of beer annually.

MASSACHUSETTS

Jack's Abby Brewing, Framingham

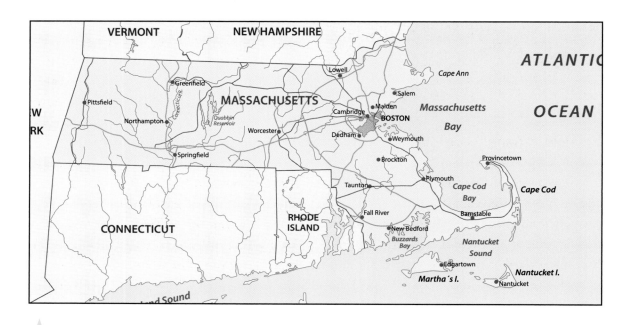

★ ORIGIN

Jack's Abby Brewing is owned and operated by three brothers—Sam, Jack, and Eric Hendler. The three have been working together since they were just young boys, all gainfully employed at their grandfather and father's business, the Saxony Ice Company. They grew up in an entrepreneurial home, learning the business every step of the way, and so it was only natural that when they got older they would go into business together.

Though the brewery was officially opened in 2011, the foundations for beer brewing were set almost a decade earlier, when Jack began home brewing. The hobby of beer making took such a hold of the young man that he eventually focused his collegiate years on learning all

WHY THEY ARE AMONG THE BEST

Jack's Abby focuses exclusively on making lagers. These differ from ales in that the fermentation process takes place at a lower temperature—lagers ferment in a cold environment, while ales ferment in a warm one. The process to turn the wort into an alcoholic beverage can take much longer with lagers—sometimes three times as long. The resulting beer has a much cleaner, crisper flavor. The pale lager is the most commonly brewed sort, but pilsners, bocks, dopplebocks, and Marzen/Oktoberfest beers are all also types of lagers.

In the craft beer world, there is a distinctive focus on ales over lagers. Sure, many if not most breweries put out an Oktoberfest or a pilsner, but far and away the ale is better represented. Jack's Abby takes the path less traveled, putting out only unfiltered and preservative-free lagers. They have carved out a niche for themselves, and with a bit of a chip on their shoulder, they have taken on the mantle of proving to the world that lagers can be just as intriguing as ales. Okay, Jack. We're intrigued.

Jack's Abby currently puts out forty-six different beers, five year-round and the others as seasonal or special releases. Some favorites are Jabby Brau (pilsner, 4.5%

he could, earning his diploma in brewing technology in 2007.

The name of the brewery is an homage to Jack's wife, Abby. Of course, it also invokes images of bald-pated monks scampering around a peaceful cloister, their dark brown robes dragging against the grass as they carry sacks of barley and hops between storerooms and brewery tanks. The brothers have taken this image to heart, following the traditions the monks created for brewing their beers—namely using local ingredients, being respectful to those who make the beer, and using quality recipes to brew only the finest of beers.

ABV, 20 IBU), Smoke & Dagger (smoked schwarzbier, 5.8% ABV, 25 IBU), Hoponius Union (India pale lager, 6.7% ABV, 65 IBU), Mass Rising (hoppy lager, 8.0% ABV, 100 IBU), Framingham Lager (June release, 4.5% ABV), Leisure Time Lager (wheat lager, 4.8% ABV, 15 IBU), Ginger & Juice (spiced India pale lager, July release, 6.0% ABV, 60 IBU), Berliner-Style Lager (July release, 3.5% ABV), Barrel-Aged Framinghammer (bourbon barrel–aged dark lager, June release, 10.0% ABV, 55 IBU), Cocoa-Nut Barrel-Aged Framinghammer (bourbon barrel–aged dark lager, July release, 10.0% ABV, 55 IBU), PB&J Barrel-Aged Framinghammer (bourbon barrel–aged dark lager, July release, 10.0% ABV, 55 IBU), Coffee Barrel-Aged Framinghammer (bourbon barrel–aged dark lager, June release, 10.0% ABV, 55 IBU), Vanilla Barrel-Aged Framinghammer (bourbon barrel–aged dark lager, June release, 10.0% ABV, 55 IBU), Cherry Barrel-Aged Berliner Braun (dark sour lager, 5.5% ABV, 40 IBU), Session Rye IPL (May release, 3.8% ABV, 40 IBU), Cascadian Schwarzbier (hoppy black lager, March release, 6.8% ABV, 70 IBU), Smoked Märzen (February release), Saxonator (dopplebock, January release, 8.5% ABV, 25 IBU), Barrel-Aged Saxonator (barrel-aged dopplebock, release TBD, 9.0% ABV, 25 IBU), and Hopstitution (super-special release).

AROUND THE STATE

Cambridge Brewing Company, Cambridge

Cambridge Brewing Company was founded in 1989. The creators' vision was to make great beer to be served at their great restaurant. To that end, for twenty-two years, they focused exclusively on being a draft-only brewpub. But over the years, people began to pester them about putting their beers in bottles. Customers wanted to enjoy the innovative, creative flavors of CBC at home, not just in the pub. Finally, in 2011, the owners gave in, starting what they now call the "CBC Bottling Project." They run their bottling schedule similarly to the way they produce beer for the brewpub—meaning there are two regular releases and a series of rotating flavors that change based on the seasons and best available ingredients. Their two regular releases are Tripel Threat (Belgian-style tripel, 10.0% ABV) and The Audacity of Hops (double IPA, 8.5% ABV, 70+ IBU).

Clown Shoes, Boston

If you have not tried Clown Shoes beer, then drop what you are doing right now and go out and find one. If you have already tried their beer, then drop what you are doing and go out and get another. As you can infer from the name, this brewery brings the fun. From the culinary flavor pairings the brewers choose to the names of their beers (and brewery) all the way down to the art on the labels, everything is cool, engaging, irreverent, and, well, just plain fun. Do you have that beer yet? What are you waiting for?

Massachusetts

➥ State capital: Boston

➥ The Fig Newton was named after the town of Newton, Massachusetts.

➥ The first subway system in the United States was built in Boston in 1897.

➥ Massachusetts weighs in at sixteenth in craft breweries with a total of fifty-seven.

➥ There are 4.9 million persons in the state of legal drinking age, the average one of whom consumes 26.2 gallons of beer annually.

MICHIGAN

Jolly Pumpkin Artisan Ales, Dexter

ORIGIN

How do you feel about sour ale? The citrusy, pucker-inducing liquid can be a bit of an acquired taste, or something that just reaches out and grabs hold of you the first time you try it. No matter your opinion on it, one thing is for sure—there are not that many brewers making oak-aged beer.

Enter Jolly Pumpkin. Founded in 2004 by Ron and Laurie Jeffries, it started its 100 percent oak-aged sour beer brewing odyssey in a 4,000-square-foot space and launched right into making the delicious liquid. The Jeffrieses didn't know at the time how popular aged ales would be. It was a gamble, considering that at the time there were very few sour ales available, and the market was effectively untested.

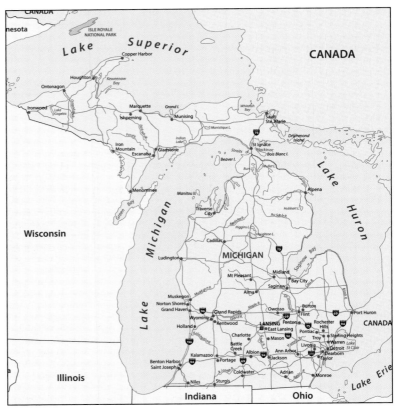

At first, they didn't sell very much, but over time, the taste was slowly acquired by more and more beer enthusiasts—those not afraid of a new experience. In 2004, they sold 160 barrels of sour beer, but by 2013

that number grew to somewhere between 4,000 and 5,000 barrels. To give you an idea, a typical beer barrel in the United States holds 31 gallons. So we're talking about more than 125,000 gallons of beer.

To accommodate all of that growth, the brewery naturally had to expand—both in space and into new products. Today, it has a 48,000-square-foot facility that produces both sour ales and regular craft beer, which the brewers bottle in a different brewery. They also serve both types at one of their two brewpubs, both also located in Michigan.

WHY THEY GET THE NOD

Jolly Pumpkin's brewers take a very traditional approach to maturing beer. Obviously, their philosophy of making exclusively barrel-aged beers means that they forgo the methods used by most other modern breweries—namely, to age their beers for a very short time in stainless steel containers. Instead, Jolly Pumpkin uses the much more labor-intensive method of aging their beers in oak casks. As the temperature in the

warehouse slowly fluctuates, the liquid inside the barrels is forced in and then back out of the porous wood grain. This movement in and out of the wood imparts another layer of flavor to the beer, adding depth and character. If the barrel has been used before to age another alcohol, say whiskey or wine, then some residual flavor from that previous aging will then add another subtle layer to the mix, making for a far more complex flavor profile and a much more exciting tasting experience.

In addition to barrel-aging, Jolly Pumpkin bottle conditions all of its beers, meaning that the brewers add a small amount of yeast in with the beer after it's bottled, kicking off another fermentation cycle. This creates natural carbonation, as well as consuming the excess oxygen that got mixed in during the transfer into the bottle. It's these time-consuming steps that help make Jolly Pumpkin stand out from the crowd.

Jolly Pumpkin makes several year-round beers: Oro de Calabaza (strong golden ale, 8.0% ABV), La Roja (red ale, 7.2% ABV), Bam Bière (saison, 4.5% ABV), Bam Noire (dark farmhouse ale, 4.3% ABV), and Calabaza Blanca (witbier, 4.8% ABV). The company also produces a whole slew of seasonal beers, which come out nearly every month over the course of the year.

AROUND THE STATE

■ Bell's Brewery, Kalamazoo

Founded in 1985, Bells's first batch of beer was brewed in a 15-gallon soup kettle. Still, in 1986 the brewery managed to pump out 135 barrels of beer—or 4,185 gallons of beer. Its production has grown substantially since then. In 2010, the brewery was ranked eighth among American craft brewers in total volume of beer produced. In 2011, it sold enough beer to become one of the top ten nationwide in total craft beer sold in grocery stores by volume. And in 2013, it brewed and packaged 248,000 barrels—or 7.68 million gallons—of beer.

Founders Brewing Company, Grand Rapids

Founders offers five packaged year-round beers, including the always popular All Day IPA, which packs all the flavor of a hoppy IPA into a session-sized 4.7% ABV, making it an ideal beer for long afternoons of drinking. The brewers have three tap-only year-round beers as well, two of which are nitrogen-infused drafts. They produce three seasonals, four specialty beers, and another four limited releases, which includes their KBS—a high-octane stout (11.2% ABV) brewed with coffee and chocolate and then cave-aged in an oak bourbon barrel. From time to time, they release a new beer in their Backstage Series. These beers are very limited, have no set schedule, and really represent a labor of love from the brewery. If you can lay your hands on some, it will be worth the effort.

Michigan

➡ State capital: Lansing

➡ Nickname: The Great Beer State (due to Michigan having the fifth most breweries, microbreweries, and brewpubs in the nation)

➡ Best month: July is officially Michigan Craft Beer Month, deemed so by a joint resolution of the Michigan State House of Representatives and Senate.

➡ There are 7.2 million persons of legal drinking age in the state of Michigan, the average one of whom consumes 26.8 gallons of beer per year.

MINNESOTA

Surly Brewing Company, Minneapolis

⭐ ORIGIN

Our Surly story begins, of course, with a protagonist. His name is Omar Ansari, and in 1994 he received a home-brew kit as a gift. His love of beer had started at the age of fourteen with a trip to the Hofbräuhaus in Munich. (Fun fact: My love of beer also started at that Hofbräuhaus, at the age of fifteen—but that's completely irrelevant.) Omar brewed batches of beer on a regular basis for many years, trying out new styles and techniques. The call of the brew was loud in his ears, and in 2004 he enrolled at the American Brewers Guild, honing his skills, learning from the masters, and eventually serving an internship at the New Holland Brewery in Michigan. By the end of 2005 he had accumulated the knowledge, the equipment, and the space to begin his long, glorious journey into the amber seas of craft beer brewing.

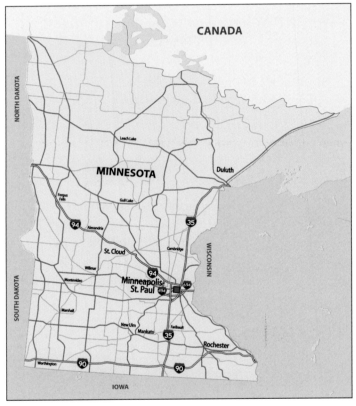

But like every good story with a protagonist, this one includes a challenge for our hero to overcome. In February 2011, Surly Brewing decided it wanted to open a brewpub. The plan was to both increase overall output to somewhere near 100,000 barrels and add a place where the thirsty masses could come enjoy the company's beer in the shade of the brewery itself. You know, like you do. As it turned out, however, Minnesota liquor laws did not allow for a brewery to offer beer for retail sale, nor could the brewers sell beer on brewery premises.

Our protagonist was up against a wall, but then, the Surly Nation arrived. The brewery had become so popular among local beer drinkers that it had accumulated a large number of loyal, dedicated fans. Hearing about the plight of the brewery, and that the liquor laws might deprive them of the opportunity to enjoy their favorite beer on the premises of their favorite brewery, fans swung into action. They made phone calls, held meetings, drank good beer, and lobbied their local lawmakers. Their efforts were tremendously effective, and within a few short months, the "Surly Bill" was signed into law, opening the way for Omar and his Surly Brewing Company to open the brewpub and expand their production.

And with beer in hand, we all lived happily ever after.

WHY THEY ARE SO DAMN GOOD

Our Surly protagonist has a philosophy about brewing beer that we can get behind. It's simple: Brew beer styles that aren't easy to find in your market; use the best ingredients you can find; and above all, brew beer you would want to drink yourself. If you are passionate enough about the beer you drink, that passion will overflow into the beer you brew.

The Surly Brewing Company offers six year-round brews: Furious (American IPA, 6.2% ABV, 99 IBU), Bender (American oatmeal brown ale, 5.1% ABV, 45 IBU), Coffee Bender (coffee American oatmeal brown ale, 5.1% ABV, 45 IBU), CynicAle (Belgian-style pale ale, 6.6% ABV, 33 IBU), Overrated (West Coast India pale ale, 7.3% ABV, 69 IBU), and Hell (helles lager, 4.5% ABV, 20 IBU). In addition, they have twelve seasonal releases: Abrasive Ale, AKA 16 Grit, D.V.D.A. (double oat IPA, late December to March release, 9.0% ABV, 120 IBU), SurlyFest (not-a-German-style Oktoberfest, September release, 6.0% ABV, 34 IBU), Bitter Brewer (not really a British bitter, May to August release, 4.1% ABV, 37 IBU), Darkness (Russian imperial stout, October release, 9.8% ABV, 85 IBU), Smoke (oak-aged smoked Baltic porter, November release, 9.5% ABV, 50 IBU), Mild (English brown ale, February release, 4.0% ABV, 21 IBU), Schadenfreude (oak-aged German-style dunkel, April release, 5.0% ABV, 25 IBU), Wet (West Coast India pale ale, September release, 7.5% ABV, 90 IBU), Pentagram (sour dark ale, March release, 6.66% ABV, 14 IBU), Damien (American black ale, 5.0% ABV, 35 IBU), Eight Ale (oat wine-style ale), and Blakkr (imperial black IPA, February release, 9.99% ABV, 85 IBU).

AROUND THE STATE

Summit Brewing Company, St. Paul

On October 3, 1983, Mark Stutrud, the founder of the Summit Brewing Company, received a letter from the executive secretary of the Brewers Association of America. The letter was in response to one Mark himself had sent to the guild, asking for an application for membership. In his initial letter, he had explained that he was working on a feasibility study to determine if establishing a microbrewery in the Twin Cities would make sense. The response he got from the association was this: "Please know that I am not encouraging you to do so, because it is a long and hard road that you are planning to go down." The letter is now proudly displayed in the brewery. Three years later, in 1986, the company released its first two beers, EPA and Great Northern Porter. Today, Summit offers six year-round beers, five seasonals, two limited releases, and one draught-only brew, and makes some of the best beer in the country.

Saint Paul Brewing, St. Paul

The Saint Paul Brewing company has some big shoes to fill. As of 2014, the company moved its brewing facility into three newly renovated buildings that used to house Hamm's Brewery. Yes, that Hamm's. Though Hamm's took up nearly 4 acres and at one point was the fifth-largest brewery in the US, Saint Paul Brewing is proud to be one of the first craft beer brewers in Minnesota. Today, the company keeps four flagship beers on tap: Railroad Island APA, Hidden Passage IPA, Golden Horses Blonde Ale, and Crooks' Haven Rye Porter. There are also seven rotating seasonal beers: Arbeer Red Ale, Festive Vest Winter-Spiced Ale, 8th Dimension Kettle Sour, Dubbel Agent Belgian Dubbel, Mosaic Passion Fruit Session Ale, Big Money Bourbon Barrel–Aged Porter, and Eastside Double IPA.

Minnesota

➡ State capital: St. Paul

➡ The city of Minneapolis has an elevated "skyway" walkway system that connects fifty-two blocks (nearly five miles) of the downtown corridor, making it possible for people to live, work, shop, eat, and stroll around town without having to go outside—something you might think about if you have to live through a Minnesota winter.

➡ Minnesota is ranked twenty-first among all states for number of breweries per capita, with a grand total of fifty-two.

➡ There are 3.9 million persons of legal drinking age in the state, the average one of whom consumes 28.5 gallons of beer each year.

MISSISSIPPI

Lazy Magnolia Brewing Company, Kiln

ORIGIN

Lazy Magnolia Brewing Company was founded in 2003 by Mark and Leslie Henderson. Leslie, the brewer in the family, enrolled in and graduated from the American Brewers Guild brewing school in 2004 and went on to apprentice at the Crescent City Brewhouse. The pair then brewed their first batch of beer for their newly created business in 2005, releasing it on the world in kegs in March of that year. It is the oldest packaging brewery in Mississippi, and it was the first one to establish itself since that darkest of dark times in American history known as Prohibition.

The brewery briefly shut down right after Hurricane Katrina ripped through the belly of America in September 2005. The disaster claimed the founders' home and forced the brewery to regroup. But

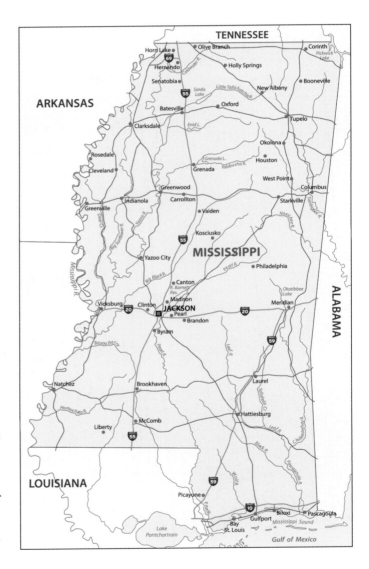

they were back brewing and distributing their beer again before the end of the year. Their operation grew rapidly as word of the tastiness of their beer spread. Then in December 2007 they took the next step,

putting their beer in bottles. Now able to distribute their elixir to the thirsty masses both at home and in bars, they set their sights on world domination—or maybe just quenching the thirsts of the beerly devoted all across the South. Same thing.

WHY THEY ARE SO GOOD

The folks at Lazy Magnolia are anything but lazy. Their beers focus on the ingredients that epitomize their home in Mississippi. It's not just about making good beer but about building a community, about taking pride in their heritage, and about presenting something new to the craft beer world. It's this spirit that is the core of the new brew movement, and we applaud them for advancing the cause.

Lazy Magnolia offers six year-round brews: Southern Pecan (pecan nut brown ale, 4.39% ABV, 19 IBU), Indian Summer (wheat ale, 4.68% ABV, 16 IBU), Jefferson Stout (sweet potato cream stout, 4.65% ABV, 22 IBU), Southern Gold (golden honey ale, 4.55% ABV, 21 IBU), Timber Beast (rye pale ale, 8.9% ABV, 80 IBU), and Southern Hops'pitality (IPA, 6.0% ABV, 60 IBU). They also have four seasonal releases: Lazy Saison (Belgian-style ale, spring release, 8.9% ABV, 20 IBU), Backwoods Belgian (Belgian-style golden ale, summer release, 8.51% ABV, 25 IBU), Me & The

Dev-Ale (strong ale, fall release, 8.0% ABV, 60 IBU), and Black Creek (imperial stout, winter release, 8.5% ABV, 55 IBU). Also available are two limited releases in their Debutante Series: Song of the South (Berliner weisse, 3.2% ABV, 4 IBU) and Old Money (bourbon barrel–aged sour imperial stout, 8.1% ABV, 20 IBU).

AROUND THE STATE

Mayhew Junction Brewing Company, Starkville

Mayhew Junction Brewing Company is the kind of place where, when you walk in and sit down, you might just be sitting next to one of the founders. It might even be Jean or Derek who pours you your beer and hangs around a bit to chat about beer or brewing. It's an easy, comfortable place with easy, comfortable beer. Today they feature four beers: Mayhew Mild (English mild ale, 4.3% ABV, 16 IBU), Mayhew Pale (American pale ale, 5.5% ABV, 40 IBU), Mayhew Weiss (German hefeweizen, 4.8% ABV, 10 IBU), and Chocolate Hookup (milk stout, 7.1% ABV, 22 IBU).

Southern Prohibition Brewing, Hattiesburg

Southern Prohibition Brewing opened its doors in April 2013. The warehouse where the brewers make and store their beer was constructed in 1941. Its original purpose was a furniture showroom. I can only assume it's much happier as a brewery. The space houses a twenty-barrel brewhouse and four forty-barrel fermenters, making the facility capable of pumping out a delicious 3,000 barrels of beer each year. Southern Prohibition offers four

year-round releases: Devil's Harvest (American pale ale, 5.8% ABV, 60 IBU), Suzy B (dirty blonde ale, 5.0% ABV, 20 IBU), Mississippi Fire Ant (imperial red ale, 8.0% ABV, 80 IBU), and Jack the Sipper (English ESB, 5.3% ABV, 45 IBU), as well as a handful of seasonal and limited-release beers.

Mississippi

➡ State capital: Jackson

➡ Mississippi was admitted to the Union on December 10, 1817, making it the twentieth state in America.

➡ The name of the state is a derivative of "Mici Zibi," Ojibwa words meaning "gathering of waters" or "great river."

➡ There are 2.1 million persons of legal drinking age in the state, the average one of whom consumes 33.9 gallons of beer per year.

MISSOURI

Boulevard Brewing Company, Kansas City

ORIGIN

Boulevard Brewing got started in 1989. Construction on the facility, however, began a year earlier, when Boulevard founder John McDonald began retrofitting a turn-of-the-century brick building on Southwest Boulevard in Kansas City. To get started, John bought used equipment from a closed brewery in Bavaria, Germany.

His first keg of beer didn't travel very far. It was delivered to a restaurant only a few blocks away. Boulevard didn't have a delivery truck at the time, so the employees just loaded the keg into the back of John's pickup truck.

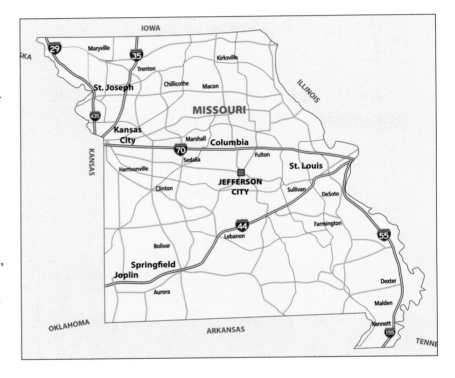

Demand for their beers grew steadily, and by 2006 the brewery underwent a major expansion adjacent to its original space. This expansion drove production capacity to 600,000 barrels a year—a 100-fold increase from the 6,000 barrels McDonald had envisioned in the original business plan back in 1988.

WHY THEY STAND OUT

At Boulevard, all of the beers are bottle conditioned. What that means is that when the beer is finished fermenting, it is placed inside its bottle, and a small amount of yeast and sugar is added just before the cap is put on. The bottles are then stored in a temperature-controlled warehouse for a couple of weeks, to allow the yeast to consume the sugar, creating carbonation and a small amount of alcohol. The additional benefit to bottle conditioning is that most of the residual oxygen in the bottle is also consumed.

Oxygen, of course, gets in when the beer is poured into the bottle. It reacts with the beer inside, slowly breaking down the brew and destroying the taste. Since bottle conditioning consumes the extra oxygen, the beer remains more stable; its flavor does not deteriorate as quickly and can therefore be kept longer before drinking without the worry that it will go bad. It's an extra step the brewers take to make sure their beers are consistently delicious, and among the best in the country.

Boulevard boasts an impressive lineup of beers that assault your senses even before you open the bottle. The company's label designs are some of the finest in the business. Expertly blended colors with classic composition, they look as if they could be equally at home framed and hung on the walls of a jazz club or hip music venue as on the front of a beer bottle.

The brewery offers seven year-round beers, five seasonals, and a whopping fifteen more as part of the Smokestack series. The Smokestack beers (named after the beautiful brick smokestack that rises high out of the brewery itself) are bigger, bolder, and often have a higher alcohol content than the other Boulevard beers. There are four year-round beers in the series, several seasonals, and a few special releases.

AROUND THE STATE

Perennial Artisan Ales, St. Louis

Established in 2011, Perennial Artisan Ales is a relative newcomer in the craft beer world. But that hasn't stopped them from delivering bold, new, and unique beers. Its focus is on creating brews for the—as their brewers call it—"adventurous" craft beer drinker. They offer a wide range of Belgian- and American-style beers, using locally produced and organic ingredients as

much as possible, and even aging some of their beers in previously used wine or spirit barrels.

They have experimented with fruits, flowers, nuts, and even squash. A perusal of their beer list reveals selections ranging from simple favorites, such as a dry-hopped Belgian pale ale, to unusual seasonals, like an American brown ale brewed with maple-roasted squash, the eyebrow-raising rye barrel–aged Mexican chocolate stout, or a wild yeast–fermented saison aged in French oak wine barrels with Missouri-grown wine grapes. Adventurous? Maybe. Delicious? Yes.

O'Fallon Brewery, O'Fallon

The year-round O'Fallon lineup is as follows: O'Fallon Gold (golden ale, only on draught), O'Fallon Wheach (a wheat/peach beer), O'Fallon Smoked Porter, O'Fallon 5-Day IPA, Hemp Hop Rye, and Zeke's Pale Ale.

Their seasonal schedule is as follows: Kite Tail (cream ale, April to July), O'Fallon Pumpkin Beer (August to October), and O'Fallon Cherry Chocolate Beer (dark wheat beer, November to December).

Missouri

➡ State capital: Jefferson City

➡ Residents of Missouri over the age of twenty-one are allowed to manufacture up to 200 gallons of alcohol per year without requiring a state license or having to pay any alcohol tax.

➡ In St. Louis, it is illegal to sit on a curb of any city street and drink beer out of a bucket. In Natchez, it is unlawful to give beer to an elephant.

➡ There are 4.4 million persons of legal drinking age in the state, the average one of whom consumes 31.0 gallons of beer annually.

MONTANA

Big Sky Brewing Company, Missoula

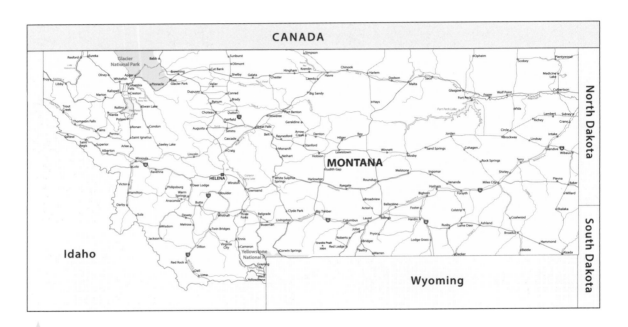

ORIGIN

The Big Sky Brewing Company was founded in 1995 by three friends—Neal Leathers, Bjorn Nabozney, and Brad Robinson. Neal and Brad had been home brewers in Michigan since the mideighties. Their bond over brewing was nearly unbreakable, cemented by their long-term friendship. The pair moved to Missoula in 1990, and both eventually got jobs at a local sporting goods and outdoor clothing store. It was here that they met Bjorn.

Shortly after arriving in their new home, Neal and Brad, over a pint of local lager, decided that there was room in Missoula for another brewery and that they should be the ones to start it. Over another pint, they set out a plan. Step one: Conquer the hearts and minds of the local

population. Step two: Find a business-savvy partner. Step three: Beer.

Step one took the form of a local cable access TV show. Neal and Brad created a new show for MCAT (Missoula Cable Access Television) called *Beer Talk*. The two men brought their passion for the elixir of life to living rooms of the beerly devoted. On the show they would try new beers, telling the viewers a little about each beer and what they thought of it. The show was a hit, shattering viewership records and setting the bar for a host of successful call-in shows that would eventually appear on MCAT.

Step two is where Bjorn came in. He was just finishing his degree in finance at the University of Montana. All that was left between him and graduation was for him to draw up a full business plan to demonstrate what he'd learned. Bjorn focused on the brewery idea that his friends Neal and Brad had been talking about so vigorously. When Bjorn finished with the business plan, the trio took it to several lawyers, revised it several times, and set out to find themselves some investors.

Step three had been in the works all along. They had been tinkering with recipes for years. They knew what they liked, knew what they wanted to produce for the market, and knew how to make it. About a year and a half after Bjorn had finished their business plan, they had collected enough investments to purchase equipment and supplies, and they finally got to work in earnest. In June 1995, their first commercial beer—Whistle Pig Red Ale—made its debut. They followed up that initial release a few months later with two more: Moose Drool Brown Ale and Scape Goat Pale Ale.

WHY WE LOVE THEM

Big Sky Brewing Company offers eleven different beers: four year-round brews, six seasonals, and one limited release. They are Trout Slayer (wheat ale, 5.0% ABV, 35 IBU), Scape Goat (pale ale, 5.0% ABV, 40 IBU), Big Sky IPA (6.2% ABV, 65 IBU), Moose Drool (brown ale, 5.1% ABV, 26 IBU), Summer Honey (honey ale, available April to September, 5.0% ABV, 20 IBU), Pygmy Owl (IPA, available February to April, 4.2% ABV, 30 IBU), Brush Tail (saison, available March to May, 5.3% ABV, 20 IBU), Powder Hound (strong ale, available October to March, 7.2% ABV, 60 IBU), Slow Elk (oatmeal stout, available September to October, 5.4% ABV, 20

IBU), Bobo's Robust Porter (available February to March, 6.2% ABV, 32 IBU), Ivan the Terrible (imperial stout, limited release, 9.5% ABV, 39 IBU), and Heavy Horse (Scotch ale, limited release, 6.7% ABV, 20 IBU).

In addition to being free spirits, and good friends, the guys at Big Sky Brewing Company make what I consider to be the best brown ale on the planet. Once you get past the image of a big, lumbering moose drooling into your pint glass, it's very easy to enjoy this beer. Many brown ales have what I call an "identity crisis." They don't know which category they fit into. They aren't as dark as the stouts and porters. They aren't as light as an amber or a pale. They are sort of the bridge between the two, and often they don't develop a clear flavor profile of their own. Moose Drool bucks this trend, standing out as an

example for all other brown ales to follow. This beer knows exactly what it is. It's smooth and drinkable, yet strong and proud. It goes well with food but can be easily enjoyed on its own. It is, in short, what a brown ale should aspire to be.

AROUND THE STATE

Lewis & Clark Brewing Company, Helena

The Lewis and Clark Brewing Company is located in a series of buildings that have been renovated and changed over the past 125 years. Their men's room used to be a smokehouse. The taproom used to be a three-story "icehouse." Back in the day, employees used the area to cool the entire building during the hot summers. To do that, they would remove ice from the river during the winter and move it up into a cave in the mountains via railcar. There it would stay until the summer, when it would be retrieved and returned to the ice house to keep the denizens of the building cool.

Blacksmith Brewing Company, Stevensville

Blacksmith Brewing Company offers five year-round beers: Brickhouse Blonde (5.3% ABV, 13 IBU), Montana Amber (5.9% ABV, 20 IBU), Panty Dropper Pale Ale (6.0% ABV, 30 IBU), Pulaski Porter (5.7% ABV, 24 IBU), and Cutthroat IPA (6.6% ABV, 48+ IBU). Its brews are exclusively available at its brewpub. If you are close enough to drop by for a pint, you will be treated to any number of special releases. There is usually more than one on tap on any given day, so sit down and stay a spell. There's a lot of beer to try.

Montana

➥ State capital: Helena

➥ The average square mile of land in Montana contains 1.4 elk, 1.4 pronghorn antelope, and 3.3 deer.

➥ In 1888, Helena had more millionaires per capita than any other city in the world.

➥ Montana ranks third among the states in craft breweries with a total of thirty-nine.

➥ There are just 741,000 persons of legal drinking age in Montana, the average one of whom consumes 41.0 gallons of beer annually, ranking them third in the nation behind New Hampshire and North Dakota.

NEBRASKA

Nebraska Brewing Company, Papillion

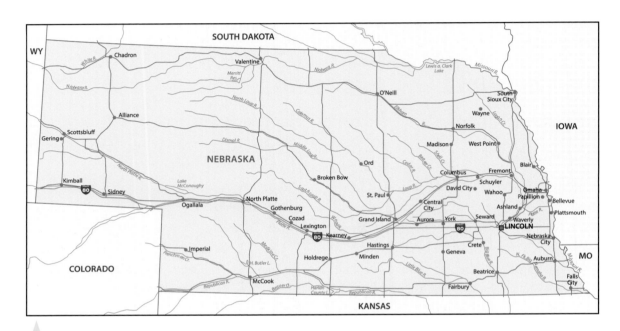

⭐ ORIGIN

The Nebraska Brewing Company was founded in November 2007 by husband and wife team Kim and Paul Kavulak. Their journey toward owning and opening a brewpub and distributing brewery started in 1992 when Paul began home brewing. Like many who catch the home-brew bug, Paul's passion for creating great beer

expanded beyond the amount of space he had in his home. It's at this point that many a beer enthusiast looks in the mirror and asks the reflection staring back, "Can I be happy with anything less than a fifty-barrel brewing system?"

Paul, of course, realized that the answer to this question was, well, no. He enrolled in the Siebel Institute in Chicago, and took his brewing education to the next level. By

2005 he had tinkered with and perfected the recipe for his Cardinal Pale Ale, making a product that he felt surpassed the other beers he could buy locally. It was time to swoop into action. Kim and Paul recruited Tyson Arp to be their lead brewer, found themselves a location and a chef who could pair good food with their great beer, and the Nebraska Brewing Company was born.

WHY THEY ARE SO GOOD

The fine folks at Nebraska Brewing Company strive every day to make their beers just a little bit better than they were the day before. That means they are constantly challenging themselves, learning, tinkering, but also submitting their beers to tastings and championships. To date, their beers have brought home more than fifty medals. They go to these events so they can grow and learn, take in the trends and the innovations that other brews around the country and the world are creating. But also, they go so that they can expose more and more people to the flavors and mastery of their beers. They like to spread the love. For that, we will be forever grateful.

Nebraska Brewing Company's beers are all available in bottles and at their restaurant/brewpub. The pub has seven standard beers: Ale Storm (5.1% ABV, 13 IBU), Infinite Wit (4.7% ABV, 9 IBU), EOS Hefeweizen (5.2% ABV, 13 IBU), Brunette Nut Brown Ale (4.70% ABV, 20 IBU), Cardinal Pale Ale (6.0% ABV, 42 IBU), India Pale Ale (6.9% ABV, 72 IBU), and HopAnomaly (9.3% ABV, 87 IBU). The company also offers seven beers in its Barrel-Aged Reserve Series, which are bottled and can be enjoyed now or cellared and consumed at your leisure: Fathead Barley Wine Ale (12.1% ABV, 33 IBU), Black Betty Imperial Stout (11.3% ABV, 67 IBU), Mélange Á Trois Belgian-Style Ale (11.3% ABV, 31 IBU), HopAnomaly (imperial IPA aged in chardonnay barrels, formerly Hop God, 10.6% ABV, 87 IBU), Apricot Au Poivre Saison Belgian-Style Ale (7.5% ABV, 27 IBU), Sexy Betty Imperial Stout (aged in brandy barrels, 11.0% ABV, 50 IBU), and Responsibly Belgian-Style Ale (aged in brandy barrels, 13.0% ABV, 35 IBU). In addition, there's a rotating tap of Brewer's Choice special releases—a treat for those who come back early and often.

AROUND THE STATE

Empyrean Brewing Company, Lincoln

The word *empyrean* comes from the medieval Latin *empyreus*, meaning "in or on the fire." Empyrean Heaven is the place spoken of in the ancient cosmologies where the element of fire resided in the highest plane of the heavens. This was where the gods dwelt, those beings so divine they were made of pure light.

It was a place among the stars, thought by many to be a paradise—if only you could get there. Inspired by these tales, the Empyrean Brewing Company set out to bring some of this paradise to the beerly devoted here on Earth. It started its endeavor in 1990, and has been going strong ever since. Today, it offers several year-round brews and a handful of seasonals and special releases. The year-round beers are Watch Man IPA (6.0% ABV, 58 IBU), Chaco Canyon Gold (golden ale, 4.8% ABV, 21 IBU), Burning Skye Scottish-Style Ale (5.3% ABV, 13 IBU),

Luna Sea ESB (6.3% ABV, 31 IBU), Third Stone Brown (5.3% ABV, 13 IBU), Dark Side Vanilla Porter (5.7% ABV, 23 IBU), and Collapsar Oatmeal Stout (5.6% ABV, 22 IBU).

Thunderhead Brewing Company, Kearney

The Thunderhead Brewing Company has been putting out fine ales and lagers since 1999. Its current list of beers includes Golden Frau Honey Wheat (7.5% ABV, 12 IBU), Cornstalker Dark Wheat (5.2% ABV, 12 IBU), Cropduster IPA (6.5% ABV, 65 IBU), Grail Ale Grand Cru (6.5% ABV, 22 IBU), MacTawisch Scottish Ale (5.0% ABV, 11 IBU), Schwabian Pilsner (5.0% ABV, 25 IBU), HHPP Pils (5.0% ABV, 25 IBU), Farmageddon (5.5% ABV, 15 IBU), Schaben's Pilsner (5.0% ABV, 20 IBU), Apple Wheat (3.97% ABV, 12 IBU), Oatmeal Stout (6.5% ABV, 60 IBU), Peach Wheat (5.0% ABV, 12 IBU), Jalapeno Ale (4.95% ABV, 12 IBU), and Leatherhead Red Ale (5.2% ABV, 40 IBU). Like all good craft brewers, they also put out a handful of seasonals and special releases, though you'll need to keep your eyes open and your pint glass at the ready if you want to catch them. They go very fast.

Nebraska

➡ State capital: Lincoln

➡ It is illegal to go whale fishing in Nebraska. The state is of course landlocked, so odds are no one is going to jail for this offense anytime soon.

➡ Nebraska is the only state in the Union with a unicameral legislature, meaning that instead of having a senate and a house of representatives, Nebraskans have only one house where all their elected officials debate the creation of and maintenance of laws.

➡ The College World Series is played every year in Omaha, and has been since 1950.

➡ There are 1.3 million persons of legal drinking age in the state, the average one of whom consumes 35.2 gallons of beer annually.

NEVADA

Tenaya Creek Brewery, Las Vegas

ORIGIN

Tenaya Creek Brewery is no stranger to change. In fact, the brewery itself was originally opened as Tenaya Creek Restaurant & Brewery. That doesn't sound like much of a change, until you understand that back then, in 1999, it was a fine-dining establishment, complete with a connoisseur's wine list and, of course, beer brewed on-site.

Things worked out well enough for the crew of the brewery, but in truth, food services wasn't where their real passion lay. They were brewers, pure and simple, and other parts of the restaurant were less fun and more work than they were worth. So, in June 2008, Tenaya Creek Restaurant & Brewery jettisoned the restaurant part and became just Tenaya Creek Brewery. It expanded its distribution, offering kegs of the brewers' beer to other

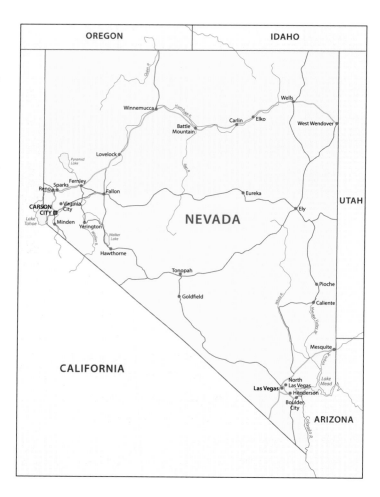

establishments (it had previously only been available at their facility).

The move was exactly what the doctor ordered, and the more people got to try their tasty brews, the more their popularity grew. In July 2010, they remodeled and expanded the brewery, adding a 22-ounce bottling line. In October of the same year, they began distribution of said bottles across Las Vegas. Today, their beers can be found in Nevada, Utah, Ohio, Arizona, and Vancouver, British Columbia.

WHY THEY'RE SO GOOD

Tenaya Creek doesn't try to be all things to all people, and they don't try to pretend to be something they are not. They know exactly what they are good at—brewing good, honest, quality beer. They don't overreach; they simply deliver solid, quality beer time and time again. They take the craftsmanship of craft brewing very seriously, and it shows in the consistent flavor of their beers.

Tenaya Creek Brewery offers twelve beers to the thirsty masses: God of Thunder Baltic Porter (9.0% ABV), Tenaya Creek Brown Ale (5.6% ABV), Gold Medal Pilsner (draft only, 5.5% ABV), Hauling

Oats Oatmeal Stout (5.7% ABV), Hefeweizen (draft only, 5.0% ABV), Hop Ride IPA (7.2% ABV), Imperial Stout (limited release, 9.3% ABV), Monsoon IPA (limited release, 8.5% ABV), Oktoberfest Lager (limited release, 6.0% ABV), Old Jackalope Barleywine-Style Ale (limited release, 10.4% ABV), Red Ryder Ale (red rye ale, limited release, 6.2% ABV), and Tandem Double IPA (limited release, 9.0% ABV).

AROUND THE STATE

Great Basin Brewing Company, Sparks

Great Basin Brewing Company was born out of a passion for home brewing and a desire to live the dream. It was founded in 1993 by Tom and Bonda Young. The couple learned the ropes of running a restaurant and brewery on the job, leaning on instinct to provide direction and making it up as they went along for the parts they didn't already know how to do. They have been in business now for more than twenty years. They have two brewing facilities, one in Sparks and the other in Reno. They were pioneers, taking on laws in Nevada that made it difficult or downright impossible to brew beer, forcing change so that they could provide the thirsty masses with good beer and blaze a trail for others to follow. Today they are Nevada's oldest operating brewery, and the most award-winning as well.

Big Dog's Brewing Company, Las Vegas

Big Dog's Brewing Company was started by two enterprising brothers from Wisconsin, Tom and George Wiesner. The pair carved out a niche for themselves in

the hot Las Vegas desert by first opening a restaurant, called the Draft House, in 1988. In 1992, they opened a second location, the Draft House Barn and Casino, a place that became famous as the city's first dining barn and Packer Fan Club (you can take a Packer fan out of the Midwest, but you can't take the Cheese Head out of his blood—I think that's how the saying goes). In 2003, they built their second brewing facility at the Draft House, and this is where Big Dog's fifteen-barrel brewhouse resides. They offer seven signature drafts at their locations: Leglifter Light (lager, 4.0% ABV), Tailwagger Wheat (4.9% ABV), Holy Cow! Original Pale Ale (5.6% ABV), Red Hydrant Brown Ale (5.6% ABV), 38 Special (a blend of pale and brown ales, 5.6% ABV), Black Lab Stout (5.5% ABV), and Dirty Dog IPA (7.1% ABV). In addition, they also bottle many of their beers, as well as put out a large selection of seasonals.

Nevada

➥ State capital: Carson City

➥ The first casino to open on Highway 91, the stretch of road that would eventually be transformed into the Las Vegas Strip, was called the Pair-O-Dice Club. The year was 1931.

➥ State Route 375, which runs from Alamo to Tonopah, was officially christened "The Extraterrestrial Highway," in honor of Area 51. The ceremony in which the name was made official was attended by the cast and director of the movie *Independence Day*.

➥ There are nearly 2 million persons (terrestrials of the nonextra kind) of legal drinking age in the state, the average one of whom consumes 35.8 gallons of beer annually.

NEW HAMPSHIRE

Smuttynose Brewing Company, Portsmouth

⭐ ORIGIN

Smuttynose Brewing Company was started in 1994, founded by the same intrepid folks who brought us the Northampton and Portsmouth Breweries. The name comes from a small island that lies off the coast of New Hampshire and Maine—called Smuttynose Island, appropriately enough. The island is one of nine that together make up the Isles of Shoals and is home to a whole host of harbor seals, the animal that graces the logo on Smutty-nose beers.

The founders first released their craft beers into the world in 1987, when they created the Northampton Brewery. The facility they built is still there today and is now the oldest brewpub in New England. A few years later, in 1991, a subset of the same

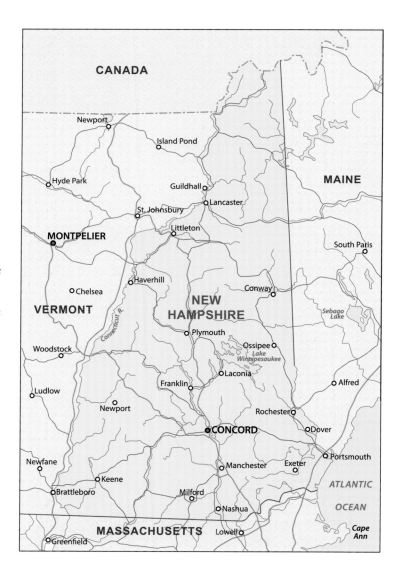

folks expanded their Northeast craft brew empire by founding the Portsmouth Brewery. Finally, in 1994, after acquiring their equipment from the now-defunct Frank Jones Brewing Company, the Smuttynose Brewing Company came into being. Their popularity grew year over year, and their latest brewing facility upgrade was completed in May 2014.

WHY THEY ARE SO DAMN GOOD

The folks at Smuttynose Brewing Company refuse to use any ingredient that could degrade the quality of their beer. To that end, they don't use any animal products in their brews—including isinglass or gelatin. Both of these products are known as "fining agents" and are sometimes used in the brewing process to remove particles that make beer cloudy, such as proteins or excess yeast. While this may only be a small part of the brewing process, the philosophy here is very important. Smuttynose makes only uncompromising beer. The brewers strive to put only the best product they know how to make into your pint glass. For them it's not about quantity or mass distribution; it's about making sure that the end product is something they would be proud to serve to their friends and be satisfied to drink in their own homes. So you can think of it this way: If you are drinking their beer, they consider you a friend. I like that.

Smuttynose offers seven "full-time" beers: Shoals Pale Ale (5.4% ABV, 62 IBU), Old Brown Dog Ale (brown ale, 6.7% ABV, 29.5 IBU), Finestkind IPA (6.9% ABV, 73.5 IBU), Bouncy House IPA (4.3% ABV, 84 IBU), Vunderbar! Pilsner (4.9% ABV, 33 IBU), Robust Porter (6.6% ABV, 33 IBU), and Really Old Brown Dog Ale (10.08% ABV, 20 IBU). They also produce eight seasonal releases: Summer Weizen (summer release, 5.46% ABV, 15 IBU), Pumpkin Ale (fall release, 6.5% ABV, 45 IBU), Winter Ale (winter release, 5.6% ABV, 52 IBU), Big A IPA (available September to January, 9.5% ABV, 98.5 IBU), Cluster's Last Stand (IPA,

8.8% ABV, 62 IBU), Smistletoe (bière de garde, 8.5% ABV, 13 IBU), Noonan Black IPA (available February to May, 5.6% ABV, 52 IBU), and Durty Hoppy Brown Ale (available January to March, 8.4% ABV, 97 IBU).

If you are lucky enough, you might come across one of their Big Beer Series brews. These are limited releases, created in small batches but sold in big bottles. They aren't on a regular schedule; some beers aren't brewed every year. They are in limited supply and subject to change at the whims of the brewers—just the way we like it. If you are lucky enough to live nearby the brewery, or within driving distance of Portsmouth, you can purchase a Big Beer Series subscription, entitling you to a case or half-case (your choice) of each of the brews that come out in the series. A subscription lasts for nine releases, and the beers must be picked up on-site. Sorry, they can't ship them to you. We know. We tried.

AROUND THE STATE

Tuckerman Brewing Company, Conway

Tuckerman Brewing Company puts out four distinctive brews: Pale Ale (5.3% ABV), Headwall Alt (altbier, 4.5% ABV), Altitude (altbier, 7.5% ABV), and 6288 Stout (6.0% ABV). Altitude is a special release of their Headwall Alt beer, brewed with the original recipe but producing a much higher alcohol content. The normal production version of the beer has a more modest kick, fitting it squarely in the session beer category. The 6288 Stout is a winter seasonal. A portion of the proceeds from this beer are donated to the Mount Washington Observatory for their weather and science exploration. The beer's name, in fact, comes from the elevation of Mount Washington, which rises exactly 6,288 feet above sea level.

Portsmouth Brewery, Portsmouth

The Portsmouth Brewery has a seven-barrel brewhouse. They brew their beers three to four times a week. As we know, a barrel is 31 gallons, meaning that in a typical week, they produce between 651 and 868 gallons of beer. They brew a staggering number of beers, not all of which are on tap all of the time. Their website lists seventy-one unique styles (complete with tasting notes, ABV, and IBU numbers) and will tell you which of those are currently available at the brewery. They do bottle a small number of their beers, and all of them are available to take home in a growler. Or, you could just stop in for a bite and a pint.

New Hampshire

➡ State capital: Concord

➡ Of the original thirteen colonies, New Hampshire was the first to declare independence from England—doing so a full six months before the Declaration of Independence was signed.

➡ There has been steady growth in the number of breweries in the state, rising from thirteen in 2004 to twenty-one in 2012.

➡ There are nearly 1 million persons of legal drinking age in the state, the average one of whom consumes 43.9 gallons of beer annually, second in the nation.

NEW JERSEY

River Horse Brewing Company, Ewing

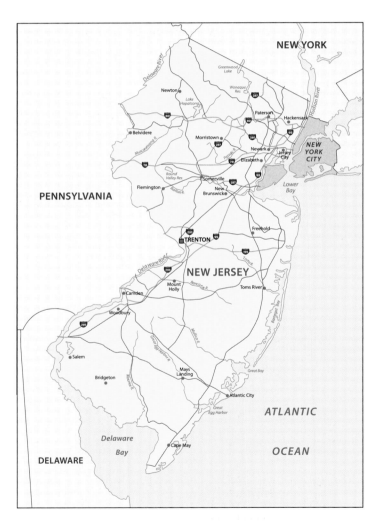

★ ORIGIN

The "About Us" section of the River Horse Brewing Company's website dishes out some sage advice. It says, and I quote, "Just remember, it's a big world out there and cubicles don't have doors, so you can walk out anytime."

As you can probably infer from that piece of wisdom, the current proprietors of the brewery didn't come to the beer business in any of the usual ways. The guys in charge, Glenn and Chris, started out in the world of finance. They wore suits and small colorful nooses—known in the business world as neckties—to the office. They sat in cubicles, and had discussions over the water cooler.

And they hated it.

So they made the leap. In 2007, they put together the money and took over the River Horse Brewery. The beer world is glad they did.

WHY THEY ARE SO GOOD

First off, they have hippopotamuses on their beer labels. You probably didn't know this, but the hippopotamus, also known in New Jersey as the river horse, loves to eat hops. I have it on good authority that this is true—anyway, this is my story, and I'm sticking to it.

Second, and more important, these guys have fun making beer. They've thrown off the corporate shackles and are doing what they love for a living, and it shows in the quality of their product. Craft beer is about the fun, about the experience, about the antithesis to corporate beer—all the things these guys are good at.

River Horse Brewing Company puts out six year-round brews: Tripel Horse (Belgian-style tripel, 10.0% ABV), Hop Hazard (American-style pale ale, 6.5% ABV), Special Ale (American-style amber ale, 5.5% ABV), Hop-A-Lot-A-Mus (double IPA, 8.5% ABV), Lager (5.0% ABV), and River Horse IPA (5.7% ABV). They also offer four seasonals: Summer Blonde (available April to August, 4.5% ABV), Hipp-O-Lantern (imperial pumpkin ale, October release, 8.5% ABV), Belgian Freeze (dark Belgian ale, available October to December, 8.0% ABV), and Oatmeal Milk Stout (available December to February, 6.7% ABV).

If you are looking for something a little more edgy, and you happen to be in the neighborhood, you can drop by the brewery and try one of their barrel-aged beers or something from their Brewer's Reserve series. Both are limited production and change regularly, so come by early and often.

AROUND THE STATE

High Point Brewing Company, Butler

Founded in 1994 by award-winning home brewer Greg Zaccardi, High Point Brewing Company was the very first brewer in America to exclusively produce wheat beers. Greg had spent time working as a brewer in southern Germany, and when he returned home to the United States, he realized that his fellow countrymen deserved to know the sweet, sweet flavor of wheat beer brewed the way nature intended it and the way the Germans had perfected it. In fact, all of the hops, yeast, barley, and wheat used in High Point's beers are imported directly from Bavaria, and their brewing process strictly follows the German purity law. All of High Point's beer comes out under the brand name Ramstein, which is an homage to a town in Germany with an American air force base and, as a result, a high population of American ex-patriots.

Flying Fish Brewing Company, Somerdale

Flying Fish Brewing Company was originally founded in 1995 as a "virtual" brewery. What is a virtual brewery, you ask? Well, I'll tell you. The company had a website (of course), where it began the process of building a community of beerly devoted who helped the owners name, taste, and, even in some rare cases, brew beer. One year later, they opened their doors for real. Today, they are the largest of New Jersey's craft brewers. In 2009, they started releasing their Exit Series beers—each named for a different exit off the New Jersey Turnpike, brewed to reflect the community and environment that occupies the area off each exit. Each of these beers is put out in 750-milliliter bottles and is available in very limited supply.

New Jersey

➡ State capital: Trenton

➡ New Jersey has the highest population density in the nation. There are, on average, more than 1,000 people per square mile in the state, which is more than thirteen times the national average.

➡ There are also more diners in the state than any other place, making it the diner capital of the entire world.

➡ The very first baseball game was played in the city of Hoboken.

➡ There are almost 6.5 million persons of legal drinking age in the state, the average one of whom consumes 22.4 gallons of beer annually.

NEW MEXICO

Santa Fe Brewing Company, Santa Fe

ORIGIN

The Santa Fe Brewing Company was started sometime in the late 1800s. Back then, New Mexico was a hotbed for local brews. These concoctions were competing with the ever-growing influence of European-style beer brewed in Milwaukee and St. Louis—the brews that would come to dominate and homogenize the American beer scene until the craft brew movement forever changed how America looked at beer. But I digress.

In 1892, the Santa Fe Brewing Company was officially incorporated, but improvements in the interstate system and mobile refrigeration technology meant that access to the mass-produced beers from the Midwest was constantly growing in the Southwest. In the face of this overwhelming competition, the brewery was forced

to close its doors in 1896—just twenty-four years before the darkest of dark times in American history reared its ugly head and shut down alcohol production in the United States for thirteen years.

The resurrection of the Santa Fe Brewing Company was begun in 1988 by Mike Levis. It was New Mexico's first craft brewery. It began with just a single beer—a pale ale—which was brewed using custom-made square vessels and brought to a bubbling head in open-topped fermenters. The brewhouse was the remains of the sadly defunct Boulder Brewing Company, which had found new life in Santa Fe. That pale ale remains to this day the brewery's flagship beer.

In the years that followed, the company's beer began to attract a faithful following. The owners took it to the New Mexico State Fair and the Great American Beer Festival. The judges took sips, sat up, and took notice of the small brewery's fantastic brews. The company added a few more beers, a nut brown and a wheat, and even more people began to take notice.

In 1997, the brewery really hit its stride. Adding a host of new talent to the brewing crew, it expanded into a new facility that boasted a fifteen-barrel brew system and a shiny new tasting room. The brewers added more beers and expanded their reach, distributing to the thirsty masses both in New Mexico and parts of Colorado. In 2005, they expanded again, moving just down the road to their current facility, which houses a thirty-barrel brewery, as well as a bottling line. And again they pushed out their

influence into other states, adding distribution to Arizona, Oklahoma, and Texas as well. In 2010, they became the first brewery in the state to can their beers, and today they are the largest brewery in New Mexico.

WHY THEY ARE SO GOOD

Santa Fe Brewing Company delivers honest beer. It doesn't try to be overly fancy. It doesn't try to overwhelm us with a mind-boggling list of brews. The brewers simply focus on their strengths and deliver consistently great beer. There is genius in this simplicity. When you focus on just the core, the craftsmanship comes to the foreground. Such is true with Santa Fe's brews.

Santa Fe Brewing Company puts out seven year-round beers: Santa Fe Pale Ale (5.4% ABV), Santa Fe Nut Brown (5.2% ABV), State Pen Porter (6.4% ABV), Santa Fe Hefeweizen (5.25% ABV), Chicken Killer Barley Wine (10.0% ABV), Happy Camper IPA (6.6% ABV), and Imperial Java Stout (8.0% ABV). In addition, the company has six regular special releases: Kriek (cherry lambic, 8.5% ABV), Black IPA (7.1% ABV), Freestyle Pilsner (5.5% ABV), Viszolay Belgian (7.0% ABV), Oktoberfest (6.0% ABV), and Irish Red Ale (4.5% ABV).

AROUND THE STATE

Marble Brewery, Albuquerque

The 2014 Great American Beer Festival Small Brewing Company of the Year, Marble Brewery, takes its name from Marble Avenue, the warehouse district in the very northern part of Albuquerque. They offer a number of house and seasonal offerings: Pilsner (4.7% ABV), Wildflower Wheat (5.6% ABV), Amber Ale (5.4% ABV), Red Ale (6.5% ABV), India Pale Ale (6.8% ABV), Oatmeal Stout (5.8% ABV), Double White (7.0% ABV), Imperial Red (9.0% ABV), Pumpkin Noir (9.0% ABV), Stout #2286 (7.3% ABV), Nitro Pub Ale (4.9% ABV), Reserve Ale (9.0% ABV), and White Out (9.0% ABV). Their tasty brews can be found on tap and in bottles in Albuquerque and Santa Fe, as well as parts of Colorado and Arizona.

La Cumbre Brewing Company, Albuquerque

La Cumbre Brewing Company was born out of a dream. Not a sleeping dream, but the dream of master brewer Jeff Erway and his wife, Laura, to bring together both their passion for beer and a desire to spend the rest of their lives doing something they loved. In 2009, they finally realized that dream, opening their own brewery in

Albuquerque. La Cumbre offers six house beers on tap at their facility: A Slice of Hefen (hefeweisen, 5.4% ABV, 15 IBU), South Peak Pilsner (4.8% ABV, 40 IBU), Pyramid Rock Amber Ale (5.8% ABV, 55 IBU), Elevated IPA (7.2% ABV, 100 IBU), Malpais Stout (7.5% ABV, 60 IBU), and Project Dank (2014 National IPA Champion, 7.5% ABV, "ALOT" of IBU). There are also a handful of seasonal and special releases available at any given time. They rotate quickly, so stop by early and often.

New Mexico

➥ State capital: Santa Fe

➥ The world's first atomic bomb was detonated in New Mexico on July 16, 1945, at the White Sands testing range near Alamogordo. It was designed and manufactured in Los Alamos.

➥ New Mexico is one of the four corner states. It borders Utah, Colorado, and Arizona all at a single point. It also shares an international border with Mexico.

➥ There are thirty-one craft breweries in the state.

➥ There are 1.5 million people of legal drinking age in New Mexico, the average one of whom consumes 32.4 gallons of beer annually.

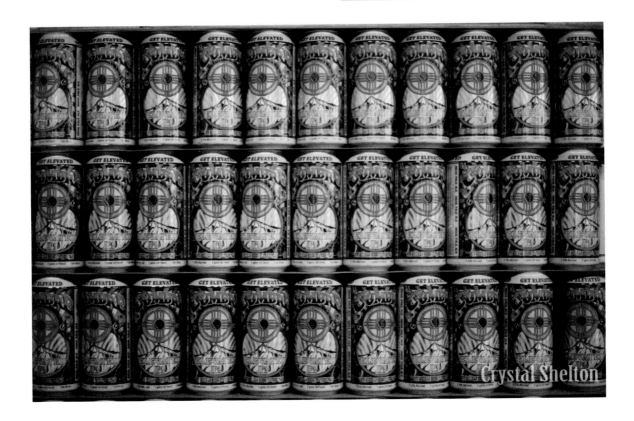

NEW YORK

Southern Tier Brewing Company, Lakewood

★ ORIGIN

Southern Tier Brewing Company was founded in 2002 in the city of Lakewood, New York, by Phineas DeMink and Allen Yahn. Their focus from the very start was on producing small-batch beers. Their first batches were brewed using equipment obtained from the Old Saddleback Brewing Company, located in Massachusetts. Their starting lineup included a pilsner, an India pale ale, and a mild ale, and by 2005 they were already distributing their beers to most of New York State and neighboring Pennsylvania.

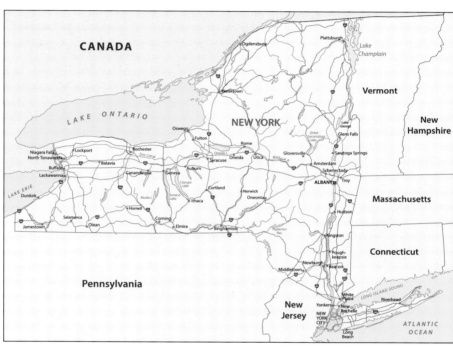

Their beers grew in popularity very quickly (if you've tried their Blackwater Series Choklat, you'll know why), and by 2009 they expanded their operations by constructing a new 20,000-square-foot building. With the new facility in place, their notoriety continued to grow, and their distribution footprint expanded as well, pushing out into the rest of the nation and internationally as well. In 2010, they added more fermentation vessels, another 800 barrels, as well as another 7,500 square feet to their facility to be used as a conditioning room. At the same time, they upgraded their twenty-barrel brewhouse to a new fifty-barrel one, and the march of brew progress went on.

Even with all of this expansion, they still couldn't keep up with the demand for their beers. So a new high-speed bottling line (capable of filling, capping, and labeling 10,000 bottles per hour) was added, and the cellar was expanded to hold 3,200 barrels, then again to hold 7,200 barrels. Finally, the owners of Southern Tier realized they just needed to go big or go home, so in 2012 they purchased a German-manufactured 110-barrel brewhouse, imported it to New York, and built their current building *around* the beer brewing equipment. They

wrapped up construction on this facility in early 2013, but by fall of the same year they were renovating again. Today, they put out over 90,000 barrels of beer each and every year.

WHY THEY ARE ONE OF THE BEST

If there is a simple way to sum up Southern Tier, it's to say that they make handcrafted beers. You can taste the love, the devotion, and the passion in every sip. Southern Tier beers are big and bold. They cover nearly every flavor profile and deliver quality time and time again. To me, these beers are like dessert. They are a treat. Something special that you break out when you have been particularly good, have succeeded at something, or just deserve to be pampered. They are smooth and easy to sip. They press all of the buttons and at times go way above the call of duty. They are examples to be held up and imitated, studied, and enjoyed.

Southern Tier offers seven year-round "standards": IPA (7.3% ABV), PMX (American pale ale, 5.7% ABV), Porter (5.8% ABV), Right-O-Way IPA (4.5% ABV), 2XIPA (double IPA, 8.2% ABV), 2XSTOUT (double milk stout, 7.5% ABV),

and Live (bottle-conditioned pale ale, 5.5% ABV). In addition, they put out a huge list of seasonals, imperials, seasonal imperials, Belgian-style beers, as well as limited editions. Of particular note are their Blackwater Series beers: Crème Brûlée (imperial milk stout, 9.5% ABV), Warlock (imperial stout, 8.6% ABV), Choklat (imperial stout brewed with chocolate, 10.0% ABV), and Mokah (imperial blended stout, 10.0% ABV).

AROUND THE STATE

Sixpoint Brewery, Brooklyn

Sixpoint gets its name from the iconic six-point "brewer's star," which adorns both their cans and at least one giant door inside the brewery. As the story goes, back in ancient times, when nomadic people began to settle in villages so that they could plant, tend, and harvest the grains necessary to brew beer, the six-pointed star was the symbol or code that represented the art of craft brewing. The symbol was present through medieval times but began to wane in popularity as it reached the twentieth century, perhaps pushed closer to extinction due to the temperance movement and

Prohibition in the early 1900s. The symbol was resurrected in 2004 in Brooklyn, New York, when Sixpoint Craft Ales opened its doors. If you want a real treat, pick up a four-pack of Resin (IPA, 9.1% ABV, 103 IBU). You will thank me for this.

Brewery Ommegang, Cooperstown

Brewery Ommegang was founded in 1997 on 136 acres of land that had previously been a hop farm. Hops first came to the New World in the early 1600s, and by the early 1800s it was a major crop in the New York area. By the middle of that same century, New York had become the national leader in hop production, churning out more than 3 million pounds of the deliciously scented plant annually. Though the region no longer leads the nation, there has recently been a resurgence in hop growing in the area. So Cooperstown, with its great water, long history of hop production, and of course its love of baseball (the Baseball Hall of Fame is located in the city), is an ideal location for one of America's premier breweries. Brewery Ommegang focuses exclusively on Belgian-style beers. Their beers can be found in nearly every state of the Union and have been a staple in craft beer stores for many years.

New York

➥ State capital: Albany

➥ Vassar College in Poughkeepsie was founded in 1861 by a man named Matthew Vassar, who also happened to be a brewer.

➥ The first railroad in America spanned eleven miles and ran from Albany to Schenectady.

➥ The first capital of the United States was New York City. George Washington took his oath of office in 1789 on the balcony at Federal Hall.

➥ There are 14.5 million persons of drinking age in the state, the average one of whom consumes 22.4 gallons of beer annually.

NORTH CAROLINA

Pisgah Brewing Company, Black Mountain

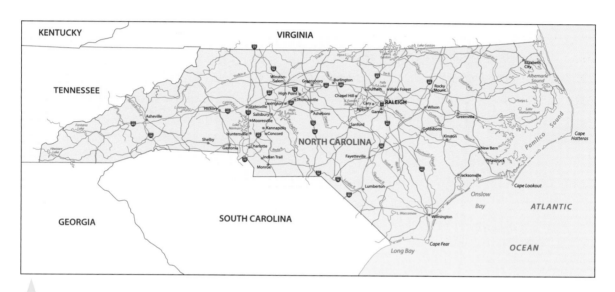

ORIGIN

The founders of Pisgah Brewing Company, Dave Quinn and Jason Caughman, met at a party. It probably wouldn't surprise you to know that they were drinking one of Dave's home brews. Two years prior to opening the brewery, Dave's pale ale had won a gold medal at the AHA National Homebrew Competition. There were 3,000 entrants to the competition, and Dave's beer came out on top. Not too shabby. With beers in hand and a gold medal around Dave's neck, the two men got to talking, and in the following weeks and months they devised a business plan.

Pisgah Brewing officially got its start in 2005. Quinn and Caughman brewed their beer inside a storage facility that was used to house the excess inventory for a furniture factory. For the first few years they were a draft-only house, selling kegs of their beer to local pubs and restaurants. They have expanded significantly since those days, moving into their own facility and bottling and even canning some of their beers. Though they have expanded their operation and adapted to the increased demand, their process hasn't changed one bit. They still focus on the details, the ingredients, and the fine craft of making beer.

WHY THEY ARE SO GREAT

Pisgah's most well-known beer is its signature pale ale—the same pale ale that won Dave that medal. Though a large percentage of the company's brewing is focused on this beer, and keeping the fans happy,

the brewers at Pisgah are also constantly trying new things—aging beer in used bourbon barrels, aging beer in used rum barrels, splitting batches of chocolate stout and adding different kinds of chocolate to each, souring beers, using champagne yeast to ferment their beers, and the list goes on. In short, they take the spirit of exploration, the essence of craft beer making, very seriously.

Outside of brewing great beer, Pisgah Brewing Company is also focused on building a community around its brews and the town of Black Mountain. The brewery itself is a major hub for live music and events. There are free concerts inside the taproom nearly every night of the week, and the company operates an outdoor stage, weather permitting, where bigger bands play and the beerly devoted can enjoy the summer weather.

Pisgah offers three year-round beers at its taproom to be enjoyed while watching events with your friends: Tripel (9.5% ABV), Pale Ale (6.0% ABV, 31 IBU), and Porter. The brewery also puts out a rotating collection of seasonals that come and go based on the season (obviously) and the whims of the brewers.

AROUND THE STATE

NoDa Brewing Company, Charlotte

Every Tuesday, NoDa Brewing Company rolls out a brand-new brew. The brewers call these early week releases their "NoDables." These are small batches, only available in their taproom, and when the batch runs out, the batch runs out. No two brews are ever the same, and the brewery has given its fans a solemn promise that no two NoDables will ever be the same. The invention and creation of each NoDable is recorded and posted on the NoDa Brewing *YouTube* channel. At the end of the year, the brewers ask the beerly devoted to vote on which of the weekly releases was their favorite. The winner is brought back and brewed into a full batch to be enjoyed on more days than just Tuesday.

Foothills Brewing Company, Winston-Salem

Foothills Brewing Company offers six year-round brews: Hoppyum IPA (6.3% ABV, 70 IBU), People's Porter (5.8% ABV, 43 IBU), Torch Pilsner (5.3% ABV, 35 IBU), Seeing Double IPA (9.5% ABV, 126 IBU), Pilot Mountain Pale Ale (4.7% ABV, 43 IBU), and Jade IPA (7.4% ABV, 86 IBU). It also puts out six seasonals: Baltic Porter (available April to May, 9.0% ABV, 51.7 IBU), Sexual Chocolate Imperial Stout (available February, 9.75% ABV, 85 IBU), Foothills Stout (available December to January, 7.0% ABV, 48 IBU), Foothills Oktoberfest (available August to October, 6.3% ABV, 29 IBU), Gruffmeister Maibock (available March to August, 8.0% ABV, 30 IBU), and Hoppy Medium Imperial Brown (available November to February, 8.1% ABV, 75 IBU). In addition, the company releases two special series, the Carolina and Cottonwood Brews, as well as an IPA of the month. The labels for each of these IPAs are designed like the layout for a monthly pinup girl, each set in an alluring yet tasteful pose. You can visit the girls and learn all their names at the Foothills Brewing website.

North Carolina

➡ State capital: Raleigh

➡ North Carolina has 1,500 lakes, ten acres or larger in size, and 37,000 miles of freshwater streams.

➡ On March 7, 1914, Babe Ruth hit his first professional home run in the city of Fayetteville.

➡ There are ninety-one active craft breweries in the state, ranking them ninth in the nation.

➡ There are 7 million persons of legal drinking age in the state, the average one of whom consumes 27.1 gallons of beer annually.

NORTH DAKOTA

Laughing Sun Brewing Company, Bismarck

ORIGIN

Laughing Sun Brewing Company was born in a dark, smoky room during a monthly poker game. Oh, how I'd love to tell you that the deed to the building had been bet on an ace-high straight, only to be won away by a king-high flush on the last card of the flop. But this isn't Hollywood. Instead, founders Mike Frohlich and Todd Sattler had finished their night of poker, during which the idea of starting a brewery had come up. Both men had brewing backgrounds—Mike as a professional, working at the Rattlesnake Creek Brewery and Grill, and Todd as a dedicated home brewer.

Their conversation spilled out into the following weeks. The two men, good

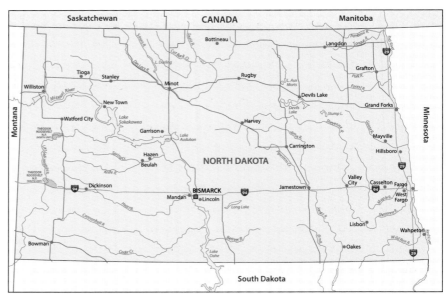

friends, talked about the idea every chance they got. Before long they were doing location scouting and applying for permits. Eventually, after they found the perfect spot, had built the brewery from the ground up, and had all the paperwork filled out, they were ready to open their doors. The year was 2012, and they have been going strong ever since.

WHY THEY ARE ON TOP

At the end of the day, the folks at Laughing Sun are artists. They are driven and inspired by the creative spirit. They surround themselves with other artists, inviting local musicians, poets, authors, and philosophers to take up residence on their stage and share their visions with the patrons and bar staff. The walls of the pub are graced with the creations of local painters. Their halls are open for all to come and share their visions. And they craft beer as if each one were a canvas, waiting for the muse and the stroke of the brush.

Laughing Sun Brewing Company brews sixteen different beers. Six of those are seasonal; the others are available more or less year-round—unless, of course, they were particularly popular and the last batch runs out before the next one is ready. The year-round brews are Feast Like a Sultan IPA (7.2% ABV, 100+ IBU), Strawberry Wheat (4.7% ABV, 25 IBU), Whippin' Post Pale Ale (5.5% ABV, 38 IBU), First Orbit Imperial Chocolate Porter (7.7% ABV, 50 IBU), McKinley Brown Ale (6.5% ABV, 55 IBU), Black Shox Porter (6.5% ABV, 55 IBU), Hammerhead Red ESB (5.2% ABV, 50 IBU), New Minglewood Wheat (5.2% ABV, 25 IBU), 107 Pale Ale (5.5% ABV, 40 IBU), and Sultan's Revenge (double IPA, 9.0% ABV, 100 IBU). Their seasonals are Sinister Pear (strong golden ale, 8.5% ABV, 30 IBU), Shallow Mud Rye Stout (5.5% ABV, 35 IBU), Irish Red Ale (5.0% ABV, 25 IBU), Black "Eye" PA (6.7% ABV, 95 IBU), Brown v. Gourd of Libations (pumpkin spice beer, 5.2% ABV, 32 IBU), and

Symphony Spice Ranger (6.5% ABV, 30 IBU). They keep a running list of what's fresh and on tap on their website, so you can decide what you'll be drinking after work while still sitting at your desk.

AROUND THE STATE

Fargo Brewing Company, Fargo

The Fargo Brewing Company, legally formed in the state of North Dakota in 2010, was created by four men. Men who shared a love of their home state of North Dakota. Men who shared a love

of craft beer. Men who, while living in their home state, took a look around and realized it was difficult to get good craft beer in North Dakota. So they took up the challenge of creating great beer for their friends and neighbors at home. Those four men were Jared Hardy, Aaron Hill, and the brothers Anderson—Chris and John. The first step was to start brewing beer. That they did. Once they were happy with their inaugural recipes, they began aggressive fundraising. Finally, in September 2011, the first pint of their Wood Chipper IPA was pulled from the tap, and the rest is history. Fargo Brewing Company offers four regular releases: Wood Chipper (IPA, 6.7% ABV, 70 IBU), Stone's Throw (Scottish ale, 4.5% ABV, 19 IBU), Iron Horse (pale ale, 5.0% ABV, 32 IBU), and Sod Buster (porter, 6.1% ABV, 29 IBU).

Bird Dog Brewing, Bismarck

Bird Dog Brewing was founded in 2012 by brewer Dennis Kwandt and his wife, Tami. By 2015 they had refined their recipes and figured out their formula for success, officially opening their doors to the public. It didn't take them long before they had achieved enough notoriety to outgrow the small space they started in. With demand on the rise, they moved into a larger facility, which currently can pump out 3.5 barrels of beer each week—and they have plans to further increase their output of delicious beer to a whopping 10.5 barrels a week.

North Dakota

➡ State capital: Bismarck

➡ North Dakota is perennially one of the top consumers of beer per capita in the United States, yet the official beverage of the state is in fact milk—not beer.

➡ There is a town in North Dakota called New Leipzig. It is known as "the small, friendly German town on the Dakota prairie." And, of course, it hosts an Oktoberfest every year.

➡ There are 509,000 persons of legal drinking age in the state, the average one of whom consumes 45.8 gallons of beer annually.

OHIO

Great Lakes Brewing Company, Cleveland

ORIGIN

The Great Lakes Brewing Company came to life on September 6, 1988. In its first year, its brewers produced about 1,000 barrels of beer, all of which were hand-bottled and kegged. Just four years later, in 1992, the brewery's beers were in such high demand that the company needed to widen its operations. That first expansion was just one of many, and by 1998 the company had taken over six buildings, one of which had previously been home to the Schlather Brewing Company. In 2010, Great Lakes invested another $7 million in brewery upgrades, and in 2012 it installed three new 3,000-barrel fermentation tanks. By the time the Great Lakes Brewing Company reached the ripe old age of twenty-five in the year 2013, it was producing over 125,000 barrels each year. These delicious suds can be found in thirteen states as well as the District of Columbia.

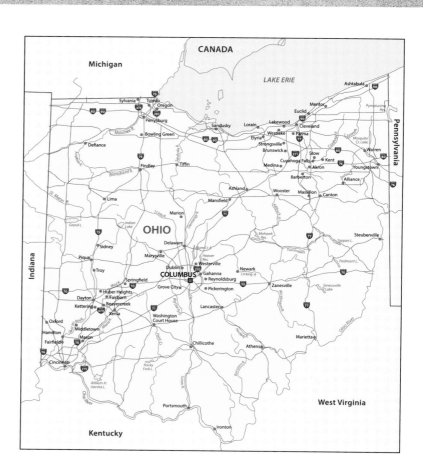

WHY THEY ARE ON TOP

The Great Lakes Brewing Company is truly one of the pioneers of the craft beer movement. Back before the turn of the twentieth century, the Cleveland area had been home to a large number of breweries. However, the combined specters of Prohibition, the Great Depression, and a slow economic recovery killed them all off. By the early 1980s none were left in Cleveland. This once fertile land of brewing was completely barren.

Great Lakes came along and opened the first—and at the time only—craft brewery in the area. In the late eighties the craft beer movement that swept across the United States was still in its infancy. Great Lakes was among the first wave of brewers to add momentum. They not only ushered in a new era of beer brewing in Cleveland, but they also helped usher in a new era of drinkability and respectability for American beers. If that weren't enough, they also make solid, dependable, truly delicious beer.

Great Lakes offers five year-round brews: Dortmunder Gold Lager (5.8% ABV, 30 IBU), Eliot Ness Amber Lager (6.2% ABV, 27 IBU), Burning River Pale Ale (6.0% ABV, 45 IBU), Commodore Perry IPA (7.5% ABV, 70 IBU), and Edmund Fitzgerald Porter (5.8% ABV, 37 IBU). The company also offers nine seasonal releases: Conway's Irish Ale (available January, 6.5% ABV, 25 IBU), Chillwave Double IPA (available February, 9.4% ABV, 80 IBU), Rye of the Tiger IPA (available April, 7.5% ABV, 92 IBU), Lake Erie Monster (imperial IPA, available May, 9.1% ABV, 80 IBU), The Wright Pils (available June, 5.3% ABV, 35 IBU), Oktoberfest (available August, 6.5% ABV, 20 IBU), Nosferatu (red ale, available September, 8.0% ABV, 70 IBU), Christmas Ale (spiced ale, available November, 7.5% ABV, 30 IBU), and Blackout Stout (available November, 9.0% ABV, 50 IBU).

AROUND THE STATE

▧ Hoppin' Frog Brewery, Akron

The Hoppin' Frog Brewery has been brewing fantastic beer for eight years. Of those eight years, 2013 was arguably the best of all. The brewery opened a brand-new taproom (which features twenty-four taps plus a special "rare beer" list) and was named the seventeenth best brewery in the world by RateBeer.com. The Hoppin' Frog Brewery offers nine year-round, seven seasonal, sixteen special release, and eight vintage specialty beers. Their year-round brews are B.O.R.I.S. The Crusher (oatmeal imperial stout, 9.4% ABV, 60 IBU), Barrel-Aged Outta Kilter (Scotch-style red ale, 8.2% ABV, 23 IBU), D.O.R.I.S. The Destroyer (double oatmeal imperial stout, 10.5% ABV, 70 IBU), Mean Manalishi (double IPA, 8.2% ABV, 168 IBU), Silk Porter (6.2% ABV, 26 IBU), Barrel-Aged B.O.R.I.S. The Crusher (9.4% ABV, 60 IBU), Café Silk Porter (6.2% ABV, 26 IBU), Hoppin' To Heaven (IPA, 6.8% ABV, 68 IBU), and Outta Kilter Wee Heavy (Scotch-style red ale, 8.2% ABV, 23 IBU). Their beers can be found in nineteen states and fifteen different countries.

Fat Head's Brewery, Middleburg Heights

Fat Head's Brewery came into this world as Fat Head's Saloon in 1992. The original location was not in Ohio but in Pittsburgh, Pennsylvania. The saloon brewed some of the best craft beer in the city and earned itself a very loyal, very thirsty following. In 2009, the brewers teamed up with brewer Matt Cole to open Fat Head's Brewery and Saloon in North Olmstead, Ohio. Their beer was so tasty that they had a hard time keeping up with demand. Working night and day, they put out more than 5,000 barrels of beer in just the first three years after opening. In 2012,

unable to keep up with the thirsty masses, they finally created their full-scale production brewery. In addition to the brewery, they have locations in Pittsburgh, Cleveland, and Portland, Oregon.

Ohio

➡ State capital: Columbus

➡ The pop-top can was invented in 1959 in the town of Kettering by Ermal Fraze. He did so after finding himself at a family picnic with a can of beer but no opener. He acquired the patent for removable pull-top openers for cans in 1963.

➡ The Cincinnati Reds were the first professional baseball team.

➡ Both the Rock and Roll and Professional Football Hall of Fames are in Ohio.

➡ There are 8.4 million persons of legal drinking age in the state, the average one of whom consumes 30.1 gallons of beer annually.

OKLAHOMA

Choc Beer Company, Krebs

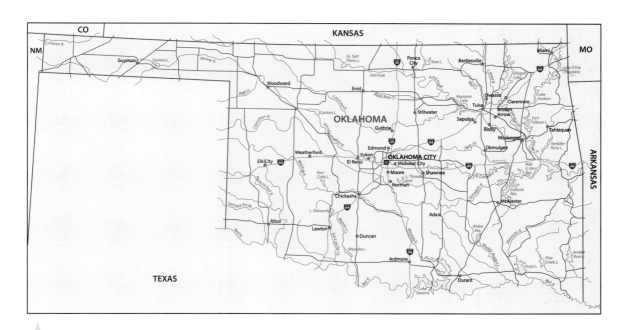

⭐ ORIGIN

The legend of the Choc Beer Company runs back three generations. Brewery founder Joe Prichard's family has been in the restaurant business for a long time. His grandfather, Pietro Piegari, came to America as an immigrant from Italy. Though it would be a tidy romantic tale to tell you that he arrived and immediately opened a bistro where he prepared his mama's secret recipes, his route was more circuitous. Arriving in the New World around the turn of the twentieth century, Pietro began working in the coal mines. It was hard, dirty, dangerous work, and eventually he was injured. Unable to continue the grueling labor, he needed to find a new way to make ends meet. As the story goes, he learned how to brew beer from the

Choctaw Indians and began serving meals and his Native American–inspired home brews out of his own home in the 1920s—right in the middle of that darkest of dark times, Prohibition. Despite being harassed by the authorities, and even arrested a few times, he continued to brew and serve his beer uninterrupted into the 1980s. Joe picked up the torch from his grandfather in 1995, adding a brewing operation to their family-run restaurant, Pete's Place. In 2004, they started packaging and distributing Choc Beer.

WHY THEY ARE ONE OF THE BEST

Any brewery that started operations in the middle of Prohibition, and continued to brew beer continuously through that dismal period—despite repeated arrests and threats from authorities—deserves a massive amount of respect. The spirit of courage in the face of adversity is something that has been a part of craft brewing from its very early days. Sure, the level of adversity has changed over the years. Brewers these days rarely go to jail for their craft. Yet, you still see brewers and their communities of beerly devoted working together to change laws and lower restrictions on the sale of

beer at breweries, or the brewing of high-gravity beer, or even the ability of people to brew their own beer at home. This is a good thing, and it can only improve the creativity and quality of beer available for us all.

At Choc Beer, they brew a lot of different flavors. Many of those are released as single-batch experiments, packaged in 22-ounce bottles, and sold until they run out. The staples, however, are nearly always available on tap at their family restaurant, Pete's Place: 1919 (their original, hefeweizen, 4.0% ABV), Miner's Light (American lager, 4.0% ABV), Peach (fruit beer, 4.0% ABV), and Last Laugh (white beer, 4.0% ABV). Drop by to check out their seasonal brews, as well as several of their Signature Series beers.

AROUND THE STATE

COOP Ale Works, Oklahoma City

COOP Ale Works offers nine year-round brews: F5 IPA (6.8% ABV, 100 IBU), Native Amber (6.1% ABV, 55 IBU), Horny Toad Blonde (5.3% ABV, 25 IBU), Gran Sport Porter (5.2% ABV, 43 IBU), Elevator Wheat (5.6% ABV, 17 IBU), Spare Rib Pale Ale (4.0% ABV, 35 IBU), Briefcase Brown (4.0% ABV, 18 IBU), Negative Split (3.7% ABV, 10 IBU), and DNR ("Do Not Resuscitate" Belgian dark ale, 10.0% ABV, 130 IBU). In addition, every year the company puts out an Oktoberfest, as well as its Territorial Reserve series: limited-release, handcrafted, one-off brews that change based on the inspirations of the brewers.

Prairie Artisan Ales, Tulsa

Prairie Artisan Ales was started by two brothers. By their own account, they started their brewery for one simple reason—to do something awesome. Indeed, at one time a hand-drawn portrait of the two men appeared on the Prairie Artisan Ales website, depicting them decked out as an astronaut and a fireman, the epitome of awesome for any pair of brothers. Their list of beers is also awesome. They offer a huge list of big, chunky, taste-bomb brews that run the entire range of flavors and styles, often incorporating interesting additions such as coffee, vanilla beans, raspberries, and chilies. They have collaboration projects with Mikkeller in Copenhagen and with Evil Twin in Denmark. Several of their beers are brewed both in their facilities in Tulsa and by partner breweries in Belgium. From Tulsa to the rest of the world, a gift of awesome.

Oklahoma

➥ State capital: Oklahoma City

➥ The world's first parking meter was installed in Oklahoma City on July 16, 1935.

➥ Oklahoma has more man-made lakes than any other state, with more than 1 million surface acres of water.

➥ There are thirteen craft breweries in Oklahoma.

➥ There are 2.7 million persons of legal drinking age in the state, the average one of whom consumes 28.3 gallons of beer annually.

OREGON

Ninkasi Brewing Company, Eugene

ORIGIN

Sometime in the later part of 2005, Nikos Ridge and Jamie Floyd, the eventual founders of Ninkasi Brewing Company, met like many brewery founders do, while sharing their passion for beer. They were in Eugene, a lovely, laid-back city in the southern part of Oregon. Mutual friends had introduced them at a local bottle shop over a glass of beer Jamie had brewed. Nikos had a background in finance, Jamie in beer. About six months later, the two men were brewing their first batch of beer in Springfield, Oregon, in the back of a German restaurant.

The two named the brewery after the Sumerian goddess of fermentation, and in

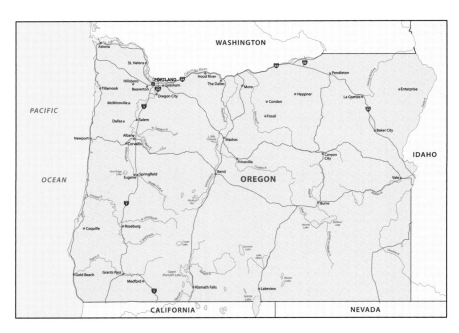

2007, they purchased the land where the brewery stands today. Their first facility had a fifteen-barrel brewing system. Today, they have a fifty-barrel system, which can put out 95,000 barrels a year.

WHY WE LOVE THEM

The core of the Ninkasi beer-drinking experience is all about the ingredients. Their beers are big, bold, and beautiful to behold. From the well-designed labels to the gold, amber, or dark brown color, to the crisp scent of hops, all the way to the gloriously refreshing or sometimes viscous first gulp, Ninkasi delivers a treat for the senses. And it all starts from the ingredients.

The state of Oregon accounts for about 17 percent of all the hops grown annually in the United States, which represents about 5 percent of the hops grown in the world. So it should come as no surprise that Ninkasi takes advantage of being so close to the source of one of the main ingredients for producing beer.

Their Flagship series of beers sport names like Total Domination IPA and Tricerahops—with IBUs of 69 and 100, respectively—and their double red ale, Believer, weighs in at 60 IBU.

In addition to the big, super-hopped ales that have become so popular, Ninkasi also offers an impressive lineup of other beers, ranging from brews that are available year-round to seasonal offerings to those that are done as part of their R&D line (Rare and Delicious).

Their Single Hop series features seven different, rotating seasonal beers, each brewed to showcase the flavors and aromas of a single, unique hop. Looking carefully at the profiles of each beer, you might think the brewers were engaged in scientific research. Each beer sports exactly the same IBU, original gravity, and alcohol by volume. Each ingredient is engineered to conform to an exacting specification, in order to isolate the variables and maximize the focus on what's really important—the flavor and aroma of each unique hop varietal.

The water that goes into the Ninkasi beers comes from the McKenzie River, which in turn is fed from runoff from the Cascade Mountains. As the snow melts, it seeps into the volcanic rock below the soil and is naturally filtered as it winds its way toward the brewery, making it one of the purest sources of water in the world.

It is said that the ancient Sumerians worshiped beer. Why else would they pay homage to Goddess Ninkasi—the goddess of fermentation? The Sumerians are one of the first recorded civilizations, moving away from a long history of hunting and gathering in order to grow crops, raise stable livestock, and stay in one place long enough to see their labors come to fruition.

The Sumerians understood the value of beer, relying on it as a pillar of social connectivity. Additionally, beer and the

AROUND THE STATE

Cascade Brewing, Portland

If Cascade Brewing were summed up in two words, it might be "pucker up." As one of the leaders in the Pacific Northwest aged sour beer movement, it certainly delivers on those words. On any given day, the company's warehouse holds more than 750 French oak, Kentucky bourbon, and Northwest wine barrels, now refilled with beers. Their brewers age and blend the sour goodness, then bring it to their admiring public at the Cascade Brewing Barrel House, aka the House of Sour, or their other location, known as the Raccoon Lodge & Brew Pub.

Deschutes Brewery, Bend

Situated on the edge of the Deschutes River, the Deschutes Brewery was among the vanguard of craft brewers who, in the late eighties, set fire to the nation's imagination and kicked off a renaissance of good beer that swept the country and returned the culture of well-made artisanal beer-drinking to America. Today, the company continues to bring good beer to the thirsty masses. Deschutes offers nine year-round beers, three seasonals (including the always

fermentation process provided potable water and nourishment—two things that were made more difficult by the sanitation issues created when a community decides to settle in one place.

Ninkasi has taken this notion of the brewery-centric community to heart. Their motto of "Perpetuate Better Living" manifests itself not only in their handcrafted selection of beers, but also in their attitude toward their local community, the arts, and the protection of the environment.

anticipated winter Jubleale), six Bond Street Series beers (named after the original Bond Street Pub, these beers explore the depth and breadth of the "almighty hop"), seven Reserve Series beers (experimental and highly enjoyable), three Class of '88 beers (brews made to commemorate the pioneers who helped kick off the craft beer movement), and three Conflux Series beers (one-time collaborations with brewers from other parts of the nation).

PENNSYLVANIA

Victory Brewing Company, Downington

ORIGIN

The path to Victory began, of all places, on a school bus. While most of us on our way to the first day of fifth grade were pulling the hair of the girl in the next seat or sifting through baseball cards or (for the youngsters) playing Pokémon on the DS, the founders of Victory Brewing Company were forging a friendship that would eventually bring the beerly devoted one of the best breweries in the world. Ron Barchet and Bill Covaleski grew up together, went to the fifth grade together, and developed their love of home brewing because of each other. After graduating college, Bill came home to find his father's home-brew kit just ready and waiting to create some new beers. He got so involved in the

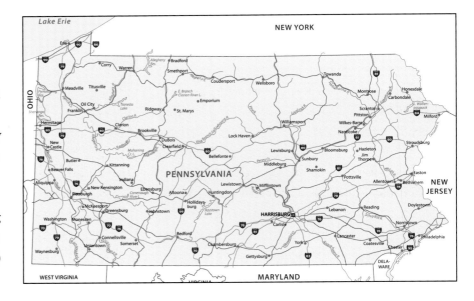

hobby that he gave Ron a home-brewing kit for Christmas.

The friendly competition between the two led them to create better and better beers. Eventually, the love of brewing grew to such proportions in the two that they both left their jobs in the corporate world and began on the path to becoming professional brewers. Apprenticeships and studies abroad in Germany followed, and finally, in 1996, Ron and Bill opened the Victory

Brewing Company in a building that had originally been a Pepperidge Farms factory. That first year they brewed over 1,700 barrels of beer. By 2012, that amount had grown to over 93,000 barrels.

WHY THEY ARE AMONG THE BEST

Victory's beers are rich and satisfying. They are bold and inviting. Victory's beers are like well-built luxury cars—everything is solid, the features are exactly where you expect them to be, the product responds without hesitation, and it just feels right. In the first sip you can taste the precision engineering. With the last sip, your expectations have risen, and they are still being met. Drinking a Victory beer is an experience, a journey toward relaxation and refreshment, and isn't that what life is about, the journey itself?

Victory Brewing Company offers twelve year-round beers: Prima Pils (5.3% ABV), Hop Devil IPA (6.7% ABV), Golden Monkey (Belgian-style tripel, 9.5% ABV), Headwaters Pale Ale (5.1% ABV), Storm King Imperial Stout (9.1% ABV), Dirt Wolf Double IPA (8.7% ABV), Victory Lager (4.8% ABV), Donnybrook Stout (3.7% ABV), V Twelve (Belgian strong ale, 12.0% ABV), Helios Ale (Belgian farmhouse ale, 7.5% ABV), Braumeister Pils (4.7–5.4% ABV), and Moving Parts (an influx IPA that changes every four months, 7.1% ABV).

In addition, they release eleven seasonal beers: Mad King's Weisse (hefeweizen, available April through August, 6.2% ABV), Hop Ranch (imperial IPA, available in winter, 9.0% ABV), Swing Session Saison (available in spring, 4.5% ABV), Summer Love Ale (golden ale, available in summer, 5.2% ABV), Festbier (Märzen/Oktoberfest, available in fall, 5.6% ABV), Winter Cheers (wheat ale, available during the holidays, 6.7% ABV), Old Horizontal (American barleywine, available in winter, 11.0% ABV), Moonglow Weizenbock (Bavarian weizenbock, available in fall, 8.7% ABV), Whirlwind Witbier (Belgian white ale, available in summer, 5.0% ABV), Wild Devil Ale (IPA, limited release, 6.7% ABV), and Harvest Ale (wet-hopped pale ale, 6.5% ABV).

AROUND THE STATE

Tröegs Brewing Company, Hershey

Tröegs Brewing Company formally opened its doors in 1996, and its first keg of beer was sold on July 18, 1997. The name of the brewery was derived by mixing the Flemish word for "pub" (*kroeg*), with the founders' family name, Trogner. The brewery offers eight year-round brews: Tröegs Pale Ale (5.4% ABV, 45 IBU), Hop-Back Amber Ale (6.0% ABV, 55 IBU), Troegenator Double Bock (8.2% ABV, 25 IBU), DreamWeaver Wheat Ale (4.8% ABV, 15 IBU), JavaHead Stout (7.5% ABV, 60 IBU), Perpetual IPA (7.5% ABV, 85 IBU), Jovial (Belgian dubbel, 7.0% ABV, 13 IBU), and LaGrave (tripel golden ale, 8.0% ABV, 31 IBU). In addition, they release eight seasonal brews and what they call their Scratch Beer Series. These Scratch beers started as a way for the brewery to celebrate its tenth anniversary, but it has grown into a regular thing. The beers are always experimental, small-batch, and available on tap in the brewery's tasting room. From time to time they package certain very popular beers, but those are also only available at the brewery. Sounds like a good reason for a road trip.

Tired Hands Brewing Company, Ardmore

The story of Tired Hands Brewing Company is one that can be summed up with just one word—love. The love, quite specifically, of beer. The brewery was founded by Jean Broillet, a man who fell in love with the allure of hops when his father introduced him to the glorious flavors of the West Coast IPAs. Soon after, he took up the hobby of home brewing and fell in love again with the subtle complexities of French and Belgian farmhouse ales. After finishing college, Jean began his professional career in brewing taking a position at Weyerbacher Brewing in Easton, Pennsylvania. While representing the brewery at a beer festival in Boston, he fell in love for a third time, this time with the woman who would eventually become his wife, a home-brewing student who was volunteering at the festival. At Tired Hands, they make their beers in very small batches, only twelve kegs at a time. The styles rotate constantly. A list of what's on tap and what will be coming out next can be found on their website.

Pennsylvania

➡ State capital: Harrisburg

➡ Hershey, Pennsylvania, is considered the chocolate capital of the United States.

➡ The first baseball stadium, Forbes Field, was built in Pittsburgh in 1909.

➡ Philadelphia is the site of the first American presidential mansion and was where Betsy Ross created the first American flag.

➡ There are 9.5 million persons of legal drinking age in the state, the average one of whom consumes 28.6 gallons of beer annually.

RHODE ISLAND

Newport Craft Brewing & Distilling Co., Newport

ORIGIN

Newport Craft was founded by four college friends in April 1999. Their first facility was little more than two empty garage bays, but it had ample space and lots of potential. After a lot of hard work that included having to cut concrete and of course outfitting the space with a brewhouse, Rhode Island's premier brewery was born. By July of that year they released their first beer— Hurricane Amber Ale.

As more people were exposed to the storm of good beer coming out of that garage, the brewery's reputation grew. In 2002, the owners expanded their facility, adding another 1,000 square feet to the 2,500 they already had. Then, in 2006, the intrepid crew ventured into making spirits, founding Newport Distilling Company and putting out a delicious elixir known as

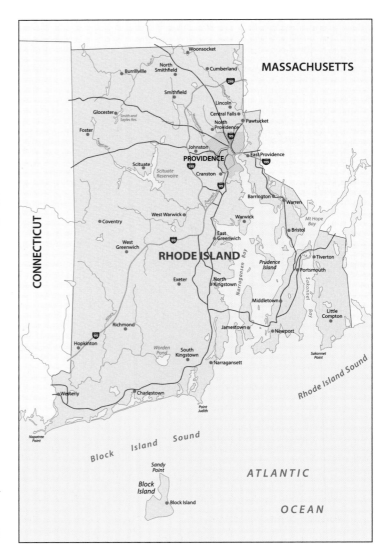

The United States of Craft Beer

Thomas Tew Rum. Finally, in 2010, they built a brand-new 8,000-square-foot visitor center, complete with a tour deck and brand-new equipment. Since its inception, Newport Craft has brewed more than thirty different kinds of beer and now welcomes thousands of visitors to its brewery.

WHY THEY ARE AMONG THE BEST

It seems to me that the heart and soul of craft brewing is very similar to the heart and soul of gourmet cooking. It's about experimentation, about flavor combinations, about bringing out the unexpected, and challenging the status quo to make something that pushes the boundaries and opens us up to new possibilities. The owners of Newport Craft strive for all of these things. Their beer menu is always in flux; they are always trying new things, treating the beerly devoted to exciting and unique reconfigurations. They lead us on a journey, one that's every bit as exciting as the destination.

Newport Craft puts out several year-round beers: their flagship Hurricane Amber Ale (5.2% ABV, 23 IBU), Rhode Trip (IPA, 6.3% ABV), Rhode Rage (double IPA, 8.5% ABV), Storm Blueberry (Kölsch, 4.6% ABV), 1639 (pale ale, 5.4% ABV), Fake Love (stout, 6.7% ABV), and Bushwick Pilsner (pilsner, 5.2% ABV). The bulk of the beers they brew are seasonal and limited releases. These include Iron Horse (barrel-aged double IPA, 8.4% ABV), Annual '19 (milk stout, 12.9% ABV), and Infringement (Russian imperial stout, 11% ABV). Keeping with the name of the brewery, they had also released their Cyclone Series, each brewed and named sequentially (like tropical storms). Only the ones named with the most recently used letter of the alphabet were available. Like storms, there is no predictable schedule for their release. But when they do arrive, be ready to grab some and take cover.

AROUND THE STATE

Revival Brewing Company, Providence

Revival Brewing offers just five beers, but anyone who's ever said a bigger beer list is better hasn't tried any of Revival's brews. Their offerings include Saison American Farmhouse Ale (6.5% ABV, 22 IBU), Double Black IPA (8.0% ABV, 85 IBU), Burnsider Pale Ale (5.5% ABV, 45 IBU), Mercy Brown Imperial Ale (8.0% ABV, 30 IBU), What Cheer? Pilsner (5.0% ABV, 18 IBU), Congo Imperial IPA (9.5% ABV, 120 IBU), Fanny Session IPA (4.7% ABV, 55 IBU), Rocky Point Red Ale (5.5% ABV, 20 IBU), Zeppelin Hefeweizen Ale (5.5% ABV, 13 IBU), and White Electric Coffee Stout (8.5% ABV, 55 IBU). Being a small and nimble brewery, Revival has the ability to react to the market and the whims of its muses, and as such, its beers are subject to change. You can find the company's beers exclusively on tap within Rhode Island. If you live nearby, lucky you. If you don't, sounds like we need to organize a trip.

Rhode Island

➡ State capital: Providence

➡ Rhode Island, as you probably know, is the smallest state by size in the Union. It covers just forty-eight miles from north to south and only thirty-seven miles east to west.

➡ The state of Rhode Island never ratified the Eighteenth Amendment, that terrible piece of American legislation that made alcohol an illegal substance for thirteen years.

➡ The White Horse Tavern is the oldest operating tavern in the nation. It was built in 1673 and served at various times as a courthouse, a barracks, city hall, a boarding house, and of course, a tavern. Though it went through a period of disrepair, it was restored in 1952 and operates as a tavern to this day.

➡ There are just over 775,000 persons of legal drinking age in the state, the average one of whom consumes 26.3 gallons of beer annually.

SOUTH CAROLINA

Thomas Creek Brewery, Greenville

★ ORIGIN

Thomas Creek Brewery was founded in 1998. They brew their beer with an eye toward creating the smallest footprint possible, meaning they recycle their spent grain by giving it to local farmers to use as feed, they collect and reuse the water from the different stages of brewing to avoid waste, and they work very hard to make sure that their business and craft not only benefit the beer drinkers in the community, but also enhance, foster, and avoid damaging that same community.

If you are lucky enough to visit the brewery, you will get to meet the two brewery dogs—Porter and Nugget.

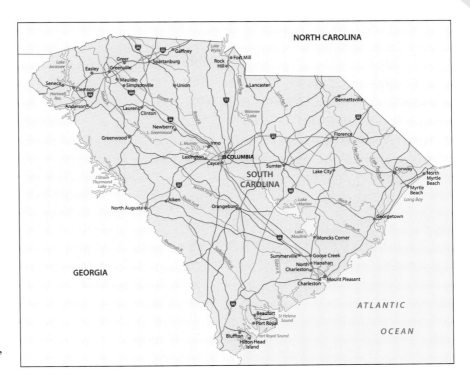

Officially, they are the "welcoming committee" for the beerly devoted who make the trek to see the operation (and for those who work there too). Unofficially, they are also in charge of spillage control and cleanup.

WHY THEY ARE AMONG THE BEST

It's no secret that Thomas Creek is among my very favorite breweries in the world. I am particularly fond of their Up The Creek Extreme IPA (12.5% ABV, 143 IBU). This is a monster of a beer. It packs as much alcoholic punch as a typical bottle of Bordeaux wine, so you need to take it easy with this fella. The first time I tried it, I drank it with a piece of homemade pecan pie. It was an accidental pairing, but it was mind-blowingly good. The sweetness from the body of the beer paired well with the brown sugar in the pie, and the high IBU balanced the whole thing out, washing it down nice and smooth. Easily one of the top five food and beer pairings I've ever experienced.

Why are they the best in the state? Because they are just good people, and they brew damn fine beer. Period.

Their distribution footprint is growing, covering the cluster of states around the Carolinas, New York, New Jersey, Philadelphia, Virginia, and so on. If you find yourself face-to-face with one of their beers, my recommendation to you is this: Buy as much as you can carry. You will thank me later.

Thomas Creek offers nine year-round brews: River Falls Red Ale (6.2% ABV, 25 IBU), Dockside Pilsner (5.0% ABV, 26 IBU), Appalachian Amber Ale (6.8% ABV, 40 IBU), Deep Water Dopplebock (7.0% ABV, 30 IBU), Castaway Chocolate Orange IPA (7.5% ABV, 100 IBU), Class Five IPA (5.5% ABV, 87 IBU), Trifecta IPA (6.9% ABV, 86 IBU), Up The Creek Extreme IPA (12.5% ABV, 143 IBU), and Coffee Oatmeal Stout (8.0% ABV, 62.4 IBU). They also offer four seasonal releases: Stillwater Vanilla Cream Ale (available March to July, 4.8% ABV, 23 IBU), Octoberfest (available September to November, 6.5% ABV, 23 IBU), Pumpkin Ale (available September and October, 7.3% ABV, 26.4 IBU), and Pump House Porter (6.2% ABV, 60 IBU).

AROUND THE STATE

Westbrook Brewing Company, Mount Pleasant

Westbrook Brewing sports an impressive list of beers, only three of which are year-round: One Claw (rye pale ale, 5.5% ABV), White Thai (Belgian witbier, 5.0% ABV, 16 IBU), and IPA (6.8% ABV, 65 IBU). The company also offers nineteen rotating brews, each of which comes and goes, a little like the tide, but sports a definitive initial release date, marking its birth and release into the wild, wild world of the beerly devoted. Westbrook has two collaborations in the works, one with Evil Twin Brewing and another with the Charleston Beer Exchange. And you can bet that the company has a brew or three aging in barrels somewhere in the deep, dark depths of the brewery. Keeping track of which beers Westbrook Brewing is currently releasing is a little like following your favorite baseball team. If you don't check in regularly, you might just miss out on the best action of the season. Drop by their website to see when their seasonal and special releases will be on tap and ready for consumption.

South Carolina

➡ State capital: Columbia

➡ South Carolina was the eighth state to enter the Union, doing so on May 23, 1788.

➡ The first battle of the American Civil War took place at Fort Sumter between April 12 and April 14 in 1861.

➡ Duncan Park Stadium in Spartanburg is the oldest minor league baseball stadium in the United States.

➡ There are 3.4 million persons of legal drinking age in the state, the average one of whom consumes 32.7 gallons of beer annually.

SOUTH DAKOTA

Crow Peak Brewing Company, Spearfish

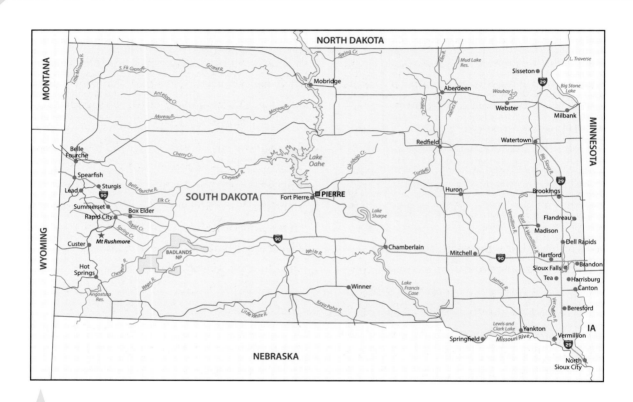

⭐ ORIGIN

The very first pint of Crow Peak Brewing Company's beer was sold in March 2007. The company started its operation with a five-barrel brewing system, focusing on producing enough good beer for the patrons of its taproom. The trouble with good beer is that news travels fast, and within three years, the taproom could no longer keep up with demand. Something had to be done.

The United States of Craft Beer

So in 2009, the brewery expanded, not only increasing the size of the taproom, but also bringing in a new thirty-barrel brewing system, as well as adding a canning line. The increased capacity allowed the brewers to start distributing their frosty concoctions to the beerly devoted in other states. They now ship their three flagship beers—11th Hour IPA, Canyon Cream Ale, and Pile O' Dirt Porter—as well as several of their seasonals to South Dakota, North Dakota, Omaha, Nebraska, and Wyoming.

WHY THEY ARE AMONG THE BEST

If you look back through history at the invention and adoption of alcoholic beverages, you can see the patterns emerge very early that eventually end up steering the modern perception of each. Wine, for example, has always been something of an exclusive beverage, being used in ancient times as a show of wealth. From the very start, those who could speak eloquently about different types of grapes, vineyards, and vintages have had a tendency to look down on those who could not. When distillation was invented, spirits became a very popular trading good because you could pack a lot of punch into a very small space, thus making it easier to transport. Spirits, therefore, were a form of wealth, and thus only available to those who could afford them.

Beer, however, has a slightly different history. Very early records show that workers and even slaves were given beer as a form of payment and nourishment. It was a beverage that could be enjoyed by the masses, no matter their station. One visit to Crow Peak Brewing and you will realize that this spirit of inclusion, of beer as a beverage for everyone, has not been lost. Sit down at the bar and you will very likely be greeted by the brewer or the assistant brewer. You'll get a smile, maybe even a handshake. And you will certainly get a great pint of beer. Beer is for everyone. Great beer is for everyone. And everyone should try a Crow Peak beer.

Crow Peak offers three "Usual Suspects": 11th Hour IPA (6.5% ABV, 70 IBU), Canyon Cream Ale (5.0% ABV, 10 IBU), and Pile O' Dirt Porter (6.0% ABV, 25 IBU). They also offer five rotating seasonal brews: Dunkel (5.7% ABV, 25 IBU), Wickedly Charming Chili Ale (brewed with locally grown peppers, 5.5% ABV, 15 IBU), Pagan Snake Stout (6.6% ABV, 20 IBU), IPL (India pale lager, 8.5% ABV, 110 IBU), and Pumpkinator! (dopplebock-style lager, 9.2% ABV, 22 IBU).

AROUND THE STATE

◻ Firehouse Brewing Company, Rapid City

Firehouse Brewing Company was Rapid City's very first brewpub. It makes its home in what was, as you have probably guessed, the Rapid City firehouse. The building itself was built in 1915 and is today on the National Historic Register of Historic Places. The brewery itself took up residence at the end of summer in 1991 and, in a mad dash of sledgehammers and reconstruction, was open for business by December of that same year. Firehouse's beers are exclusively available on tap at the brewery. The beers rotate at the whim of their creative mad brewer. The company always has at least nine of its own beers on tap at any one time. Drop by the website to see a list of styles Firehouse has previously brewed. Better yet, drop by the Firehouse and pick up a pint of what's fresh.

South Dakota

➡ State capital: Pierre

➡ The sculpting of the presidential faces on Mount Rushmore, done by Gutzon Borglum, was started in 1927. It took fourteen years to complete and cost about $1 million.

➡ The USS *South Dakota* was the most decorated battleship of World War II.

➡ There are almost 600,000 persons of legal drinking age in the state, the average one of whom consumes 38.9 gallons of beer annually.

The United States of Craft Beer

TENNESSEE

Yazoo Brewing Company, Nashville

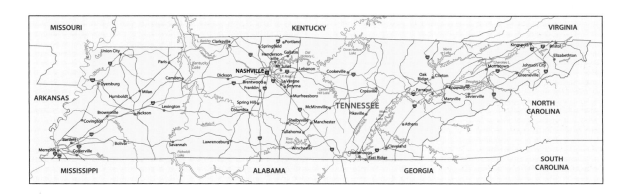

⭐ ORIGIN

You could say that Yazoo Brewing Company owes its existence to a Rolling Stone—no, not a drifter or a decrepit rock star. Linus Hall, the brewery's founder and brewmaster, bought his first home-brewing kit in 1993 after seeing one for sale in the back pages of a *Rolling Stone* magazine. He was in college at the time, and like so many beer-thirsty, cash-strapped college students have done (this author included), he started brewing his own beer. Turns out, Linus was much better at it than most (this author included). So he kept at it.

A little more than ten years later, Yazoo Brewing Company opened its doors. The company started out selling kegs of beer to local pubs and restaurants. Meanwhile, it brought its tasty brews to beer festivals, testing its mettle against brewers from across the nation. It won awards. Like you do when you make good beer, the brewery gained popularity. In 2005, the brewers started bottling their beers, and in 2009, they obtained a distillery license, enabling them to create Tennessee's first ever legally brewed high-gravity beer, Yazoo Sue, a beer they make to this day.

In 2010, they finally outgrew the space they were in. They purchased a new

building and installed a forty-barrel brewing system. They are now set up to grow into the future. In addition, they took on the task of reviving a legend—Gerst beer. Gerst was one of the jewels of Tennessee before Prohibition, but sadly the brewery never recovered from that dark stretch of American history. Thanks to Yazoo, the Gerst tradition lives on today.

WHY THEY ARE ONE OF THE BEST

Linus has completely embraced the spirit of craft brewing in America. By that I mean he's pushing boundaries, experimenting and helping to expand the horizons of beer drinkers from coast to coast. To that end,

he's teamed up with Tennessee brewer and writer Brandon Jones to concoct what they are calling the "Embrace the Funk" series. This series is dedicated entirely to sour and wild ales. They employ wild yeasts, souring microbes, and wooden aging casks to create new tastes. Not everyone is a fan of sour beers. I'll admit it can be an acquired taste for many. The funk can easily go wrong, but despite the rather polarizing flavor of these brews, there is no denying that creating a great sour beer requires true craftsmanship.

Yazoo Brewing Company offers eight year-round beers: Pale Ale (5.8% ABV, 47 IBU), Dos Perros (Mexican-style dark altbier, 4.9% ABV, 16 IBU), Hefeweizen (5.0% ABV, 18 IBU), Sly Rye Porter (5.7% ABV, 28 IBU), Onward Stout (3.8% ABV, 35 IBU), Hop Project IPA (a rotating IPA-style beer that changes recipes with each batch, 5.7% ABV, 75+ IBU), Gerst Amber Ale (5.1% ABV, 11 IBU), and Sue (smoked beer, 9.2% ABV, 72 IBU). In addition, they put out four seasonal brews (subject to change each year): Spring Seasonal (helles bock, 5.0% ABV), Summer Seasonal (wheat ale, 5.0% ABV), Fall Lager (5.5% ABV, 26 IBU), and Red House IPA (red ale, 7.0% ABV).

AROUND THE STATE

▪ *Wiseacre Brewing Company, Memphis*

Wiseacre Brewing Company is one of the newest additions to the American craft brew scene. But even though it's new, it is already highly sought after. Founded in late 2013, the company learned its brews were so popular that within nine months of opening its doors, it decided to expand its facility. The expansion allowed the owners to add twenty new jobs to the community, and now they offer four beers to their year-round offerings. Wiseacre's All-Day Everyday beers are Ananda (IPA, 6.1% ABV, 61 IBU), Tiny Bomb (pilsner, 4.5% ABV, 53 IBU), Tarasque (saison, 5.9% ABV, 41 IBU), and Gotta Get Up to Get Down Coffee

Milk Stout (5.0% ABV). In addition, they offer seven special releases: Snowbeard (barleywine, winter release, 9.5% ABV, 110 IBU), Azazel (Belgian golden ale, spring release, 10.0% ABV, 25 IBU), Avast! Pirate Porter (5.0% ABV, 18 IBU), Unicornucopia (saison), Uncle Puppy (hefeweizen), Holy Candy (Belgian dubbel), and Oktoberfest.

Tennessee

➡ State capital: Nashville

➡ Nashville's *Grand Ole Opry* is the longest continually running live radio program in the world. It has been broadcast over the airwaves every Friday and Saturday night since 1925.

➡ During the American Civil War, Tennessee was the last Southern state to secede from the Union, and the first to be readmitted when the war ended.

➡ There are 4.7 million persons of legal drinking age in the state, the average one of whom consumes 26.2 gallons of beer annually.

TEXAS

Live Oak Brewing Company, Austin

ORIGIN

Live Oak Brewing Company began brewing beer in 1997. It is Austin's oldest craft brewery, and proud to be one of the fixtures in Texas's weirdest town. Like many of the craft beer institutions in this nation, Live Oak was started by a pair of home-brewing friends. Brian Peters and Chip McElroy started the brewery as a two-man show, acting as brewers, keg washers, salesmen, janitors, and general managers. They did what they had to in order to make great beer and to live their passion.

WHY THEY ARE AMONG THE BEST

If you have ever been to Austin, you know that the city has a special reputation in the state of Texas. In addition to having their finger on the pulse of live music, each year hosting the South by Southwest (SXSW) music festival, Austinites also have a reputation for being "weird." That's not to say that the people there are misshapen, have unsightly habits, or are socially awkward. Quite the contrary. The folks in Austin are some of the nicest people you will ever have the pleasure to meet. Instead, the town has a reputation for being quirky, creative, and vibrant. Live Oak embraces these qualities as well. The company employs several Old-World brewing techniques—like open fermentation and secondary lagering—that many other breweries in America do not practice. The brewers there just do things a little differently, and frankly, that's what makes them great.

Live Oak Brewing Company's year-round beers include Hefeweizen (5.2% ABV, 12 IBU), Pilz (4.7% ABV, 29 IBU), Big Bark Amber Lager (4.9% ABV, 25 IBU), and Grodziskie (3.0% ABV, 36 IBU). They also put out four regular seasonals: Primus Weizenbock (winter release, 8.3% ABV, 10 IBU), Gold (spring release, 4.8% ABV, 34 IBU), Pre-War Pils (summer release, 5.0% ABV, 32 IBU), and Oaktoberfest (fall release, 5.8% ABV, 20 IBU). Each season includes at least two other rotating special release beers, so each quarter you can expect three new Live Oak beers to be pouring from the taps at select Texas-based restaurants and bars.

AROUND THE STATE

Jester King Brewery, Austin

The folks at Jester King Brewery describe their operation as an "authentic farmhouse brewery." They say this not only because they are out in the country, on a piece of land that may make many feel that they are indeed on a farm, but also because the beers they make are all wild ales or spontaneously fermented beers. All of their beers are brewed with water from their on-site well, all of their grains are sourced and malted locally, and their wild yeasts are all native to the Austin area. Jester King is a very small brewery, producing less than 1,500 barrels a year. If you live in Texas, are within driving distance of Austin, or have a friend who is, make plans to get some of their beer.

Austin Beerworks, Austin

The guys at Austin Beerworks love cans. No, not those cans. They like beer in cans. Specifically, they like *their* beer in cans. Why? If you asked them this, they would tell you because beer tastes better out of the keg, and cans are just little kegs. They would also tell you that the environmental impact of cans versus glass is huge, and that recyclable cans are the responsible way to enjoy your beer. They might also tell you that when the weather gets ultra-hot in the Austin summer, they really like to go tubing, and you just can't take glass bottles out on the lake or river. These are all good reasons. The boys at Austin Beerworks put out four core beers: Fire Eagle (IPA, 6.4% ABV, 70 IBU), Black Thunder (Schwarzbier, 5.3% ABV, 45 IBU), Pearl Snap (pilsner, 5.3% ABV, 45 IBU), and Peacemaker (American ale, 5.0% ABV, 15 IBU).

Texas

➡ State capital: Austin

➡ Texas actually declared itself an independent nation in 1836, and it stayed independent until 1845.

➡ The name *Texas* comes from the Hasinai word *tejas*, which means "friends" or "allies."

➡ The state covers 267,339 square miles, which is 7.4 percent of the entire United States.

➡ There are 18 million people of legal drinking age in the state, the average one of whom consumes 34.4 gallons of beer annually.

UTAH

Uinta Brewing Company, Salt Lake City

⭐ ORIGIN

The Uinta Brewing Company started in 1993 in a renovated mechanic's garage. By 1996, the owners had to put in a bottling line to keep up with the growing demand for their beers. By 2001, they had completely outgrown their original facility and relocated to the 26,000-square-foot building they currently reside in today.

The brews they make range from 4% to about 10% ABV. At first glance, those numbers might not seem significant. "Wouldn't it be more significant to describe the range of beer types a brewery offers?" you might ask. Considering the context, however, it makes a lot of sense.

Utah is a control state. That means hard alcohol must be purchased from a state-controlled liquor store. By law, any beer that is over 3.2% alcohol by weight (which is slightly higher than 4% ABV) is considered to be hard alcohol. That means

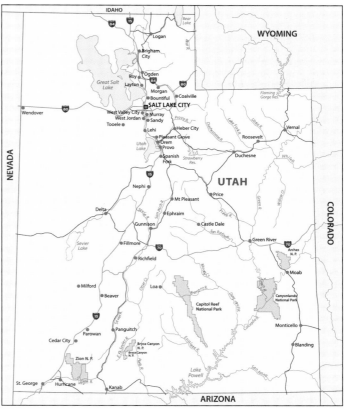

it cannot be sold on tap in a bar or pub, and cannot be sold in bottles or cans in grocery stores. So selling beers that range up to 10% ABV requires that they be purchased at stores with special licenses.

WHY THEY ARE ON TOP

If you look closely, you will see that the Uinta Brewing logo is actually a compass with the needle pointing both east and west. The needle sits just under a mountain range—the east to west–running mountain range in the northeastern part of the state for which the brewery was named. The compass, which harkens to the exploration and creativity that the brewery aims to capture in its beers, is accompanied by its motto, "Earth, Wind, and Beer"—a direct statement to the company's commitment both to the preservation of the world we live on and to creating a beverage that makes living here so much more enjoyable.

To that end, all of Uinta's beers are brewed using 100 percent renewable energy. Uinta has been a completely wind-powered brewery since 2001. And in 2011, the company took its energy effort to the next level, installing solar-electric paneling on the roof of the brewery.

Despite the challenge that is presented by brewing beer in one of the more restrictive states in the Union, Uinta Brewing has not only survived; it has thrived—continually pushing the boundaries of craft beer.

The beers are big and bold, fresh and refreshing. Uinta offers three distinct lines of beer: the Classic Line (tried-and-true releases that span from easy sipping summer lagers to viscous barleywines to session IPAs and nearly every flavor profile in between), the Organic Line (USDA certified organic beers), and the Crooked Line (special releases brewed for the curious and those who crave exploration). Their labels are colorful, simple, warm, and inviting. Their beers have names that evoke images of being outdoors, and of living life to its fullest—Skipping Stone Summer Lager, Detour Double IPA, Rise and Pine, and Birthday Suit Sour Brown Ale.

At the end of the day, the brewers put out a solid, honest product that will put a smile on your face and make you wish you had a sampler box with one of each flavor in it and enough time to just relax and try them all.

AROUND THE STATE

Epic Brewing Company, Salt Lake City

Epic Brewing Company is the first brewery in Utah since Prohibition (what many recognize as the darkest thirteen-year period in American history, 1920–1933) to brew exclusively high-alcohol-content beers. They offer three different series of brews. The Classic series are bread-and-butter beers, those you can find anytime. The Elevated series are special releases that strive to demonstrate the depth and variability that a good brewer can achieve within a single style of beer. Each batch has a unique number on the label, so you can track how the batch you are drinking changed from the batch before or after it, or—if you are lucky enough to find them—you can buy several different batches and try them side by side. Finally, their Exponential series also have unique batch numbers but are more focused on exploration and experimentation—the beers for the "ever-curious" as they say.

Red Rock Brewery, Salt Lake City

Red Rock Brewery operates three brewpubs and a bottle shop in the state of Utah. The law in the Beehive State declares that beer served on tap cannot be over 4% ABV, but that hasn't stopped Red Rock from putting up at least ten house-brewed draft beers in each of its brewpubs. The list of their draft classics is as follows: Honey Wheat, Organic Zwickel Bier, Hefeweizen, Steamer, Rye Pale Ale, Hibernien Ale, Amber Ale, India Dark Ale, Belgian Dark, and Oatmeal Stout. And every one of them is a session beer! Of course, "high point" beers (those over 4% ABV) can be brewed and sold in Utah, but only in a bottle. Thus, Red Rock offers two lines of bottled beer—Fine Line and Artist Palette—both of which are unbridled by the restrictions of their draft brethren.

Utah

➡ State capital: Salt Lake City

➡ Utah is the eleventh-largest state in the Union by land mass and thirty-third by population.

➡ In Utah, it is against the law to sell, offer for sale, or furnish beer to the general public in vessels larger than two liters. Authorized retailers are allowed to possess larger containers—kegs, for example—but only if they intend to dispense the beer for consumption on their own premises.

➡ Not surprisingly, per-capita consumption of beer in Utah is the lowest in the nation. There are 1.8 million persons of legal drinking age in Utah, the average one of whom consumes 20.2 gallons of beer annually.

VERMONT

Magic Hat Brewing Company, South Burlington

ORIGIN

Magic Hat Brewing Company's founding partner, Alan Newman, is somewhat of a serial entrepreneur. Prior to starting the brewery, he had his hand in starting a gardening supply store and a marketing company, both in Burlington, Vermont. The marketing company eventually transformed into a retail business when one of Alan's clients offered him a catalog sales company. After successfully transforming the catalog, Alan eventually got out of the retail business and into brewing. The year was 1994. The year Magic Hat was born.

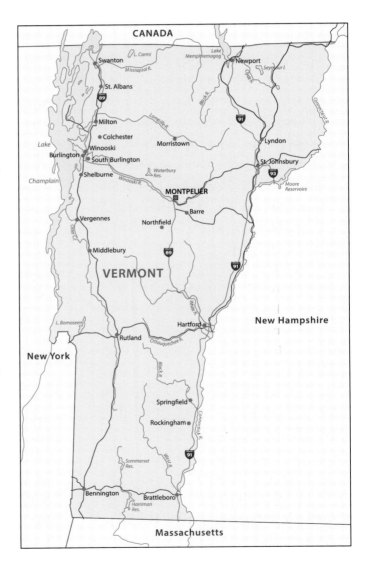

WHY THEY HAVE SO MUCH MAGIC

They do things differently at Magic Hat. When the brewery was opened, there were already several well-established breweries in Vermont. The founders, Alan Newman and Bob Johnson, figured there wasn't room in the state for another traditional brewery. So they made the shrewd decision to be creative, to not play by the other guys' rules, and to make beer that defies expectation. From the quirky name of their beers to the unusual titles of their brewery team to the unique flavors of their beers, Magic Hat is an operation that forges its own path. And to me, that's what's so special about the spirit of craft brewing.

Magic Hat Brewing Company offers four year-round brews: #9 ("not quite" pale ale, 5.1% ABV, 20 IBU), Circus Boy (hefeweizen, 4.5% ABV, 15 IBU), Dream Machine (India pale lager, 5.7% ABV, 50 IBU), and Single Chair (golden ale, 5.0% ABV, 17 IBU). It also offers four seasonal beers: Pistil (spring release, 4.5% ABV, 20 IBU), Elder Betty (weiss-style ale, summer release, 5.5% ABV, 13 IBU), Wilhelm Scream (pumpkin ale, fall release, 5.4% ABV, 20 IBU), and Snow Roller (brown ale, winter release, 6.2% ABV, 40 IBU). If you are lucky, you will run into one of the handful of special release beers, each of which is brewed in small batches and often has a unique and interesting flavor profile. I mentioned that these guys are creative, right? Pick up one of their special releases, and you'll know what I mean.

AROUND THE STATE

▨ Hill Farmstead Brewery, Greensboro

To say the Hill Farmstead Brewery is a family affair is to take the word "family" too lightly. The brewery rests on the land that once belonged to the founder's grandfather. Its logo is a modernized version of the sign that in the early 1800s once hung in front of the owner's great-great-great-grandfather's tavern, which was located just up the hill from the brewery. And its Ancestral Series of beers each sports the name of an important, loved member of the family.

The brewer at Hill Farmstead is all about the muse. Most of his beers are brewed in series, and each of those is constantly in flux. You can think of each series like a set of railroad tracks. They keep you from falling off a cliff on one side or steering into oncoming vehicular traffic on the other, but there are miles and miles of unexplored land ahead and behind, and they can take you to places you've never been before. These are small-batch, limited-availability beers. If you want them, you are going to have to work to get them.

The Alchemist, Waterbury

The Alchemist is unique among breweries in America. Why? Because since 2003 its brewers have been brewing just one beer. That's right. It's not a typo. They focus on creating the best unfiltered American double IPA they can make, week after week, year after year. If that is not love and devotion, I don't know what is. Their goal is to provide drinkers with the glory that is the flavor and aroma of that magnificent flower—the hop—without adding the astringent bite that can come from many pale beers. They make a proprietary blend of six different types of hops and use them to brew Heady Topper, their flagship, their one and only masterpiece. From 2003 to 2011, Heady Topper was only available on tap at their brewpub. In 2011, the Alchemist built a cannery in order to share the love. If you want to lay your hands on some of this fine, fine liquid, you'll need to get yourself to Vermont. Fresh beer can only travel so far. Drink it early; drink it often.

If you're fortunate enough to be in the vicinity of Waterbury when Alchemist is holding a truck sale (check their blog on their website), you can purchase some of their other concoctions. You purchase by the case (one case per purchase, though you can get back in line after your first purchase) and pay by cash. Some of the beers they've sold in past truck sales include Luscious (British-style imperial stout, 11.0% ABV), Focal Banger (American IPA, 7.0% ABV), The Crusher (American double IPA, 9.6% ABV), and Rapture! (double IPA, 9.6% ABV).

Vermont

➡ State capital: Montpelier

➡ The name *Vermont* comes from the combination of two French words: *vert* (which means "green") and *mont* (which means "mountain").

➡ The state covers 9,250 square miles, making it the forty-third largest in the Union.

➡ Vermont was the fourteenth state admitted to the Union, the first after the original thirteen colonies.

➡ There are just about 500,000 persons of legal drinking age in the state, the average one of whom consumes 35.3 gallons of beer annually.

VIRGINIA

AleWerks Brewing Company, Williamsburg

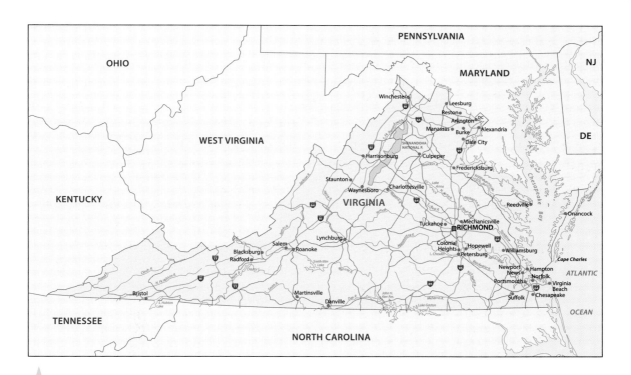

★ ORIGIN

AleWerks was founded in 2006. It is, and proudly so, Williamsburg's only microbrewery. The brewery is located right smack dab in the center of what was once one of the early New-World colonies. The brewers create their beer in a direct-fired, brick-encased brewhouse, then ferment it in state-of-the-art vessels, blending the tradition of their heritage (colonists were among the very first home brewers in America) with the modern advancements of today.

WHY THEY ARE AMONG THE BEST

We've all heard the saying "practice makes perfect." My parents tried to use this as a catchall whenever they wanted to get me to do something I didn't want to do—finish my homework, practice the guitar, iron my own clothes. My mother once even tried to use it to get me to wash her car on Christmas morning (don't ask). In any case, while the saying may have felt more like a nuisance than real wisdom when we were children, the truth of the matter is that the more knowledgeable you are about something, the better you are at doing it. Such is the case with the folks at AleWerks. Everyone here, from the brewer to the keg washer to the brewery tour guide, really knows their stuff. It's this mastery of the craft that enables them to make such great beer. That and the fact that they have hundreds of years of local beer-brewing heritage to fall back on.

AleWerks Brewing offers six year-round brews: Tavern Ale (brown ale, 6.0% ABV), Chesapeake Pale Ale (5.7% ABV), Drake Tail (IPA, 7.3% ABV), Red Marker Ale (amber, 5.0% ABV), Wheat Ale (5.6% ABV), and Washington's Porter (6.5% ABV). In addition, it has three regular seasonal releases: Pumpkin Ale (fall release, 7.3% ABV), Coffeehouse Stout (winter release, 5.4% ABV), and White Ale (witbier, spring release, 4.5% ABV). If you're lucky, you might come across one of the company's Brewmaster Reserve beers on tap or in bottles, often released for special occasions or just because the muse struck the brewmaster squarely between the eyes.

AROUND THE STATE

Blue Mountain Brewery, Afton

Blue Mountain Brewery has taken the concept of craft brewing and embraced it in a two-armed bear hug. Like a chef who takes matters into his own hands, growing his own herbs and produce in order to ensure only the finest experience for his diners, Blue Mountain's brewers take steps to ensure that they are in total control of the ingredients and their final product. All of the water they use to brew their beers comes from an on-site 300-foot well, fed by miles upon miles of watershed underneath a virgin forest. They also grow their own hops on their very own hop farm, selecting the very best to feature year-round in their Full Nelson Virginia Pale Ale. In addition, each year at hop harvest, they use the first 150 pounds they pick to brew a single thirty-barrel batch of wet-hopped beer—an offering for the bacchanal, if you will, to celebrate another delicious year of hop growth.

Devil's Backbone Brewing Company, Lexington

Devil's Backbone Brewing Company has won many prestigious awards. Chief among those are perhaps its brewer of the year awards in 2012 (Small), 2013 (Small), and 2014 (Midsize), from the Great American Beer Festival. The company offers a wide variety of beers, most of which are only available on tap either in its brewpub or in other locations in the state of Virginia. The brewers do, however, bottle a number of their beers: Vienna Lager (4.9% ABV, 18 IBU), Eight Point IPA (5.9% ABV, 60 IBU), Schwartz Bier (5.1% ABV, 18 IBU), Dark Abby (Belgian-style dunkel, 7.5% ABV, 18 IBU), Azrael (Belgian-style strong golden ale, 7.8% ABV, 25 IBU), Catty Wompus (IPA, 7.5% ABV, 50 IBU), Turbo Cougar (strong golden lager, 6.8% ABV, 38 IBU), Kilt Flasher (Scotch ale, 8.0% ABV, 20 IBU), and Sixteen Point Imperial IPA (double IPA, 9.1% ABV, IBU...yes!). They put some in cans too: Golden Leaf Lager (4.5% ABV, 17 IBU), Reilly's Red Ale (5.8% ABV, 28 IBU), and Striped Bass Pale Ale (4.8% ABV, 22 IBU).

Virginia

➡ State capital: Richmond

➡ The Pentagon, in Arlington, is the largest office building in the world.

➡ About half of the people in the United States live within a 500-mile radius of Richmond, Virginia.

➡ More than half of the battles fought in the American Civil War took place in Virginia—over 2,200 of the 4,000 battles.

➡ There are almost 6 million persons of legal drinking age in the state, the average one of whom consumes 26.7 gallons of beer annually.

WASHINGTON STATE

Elysian Brewing Company, Seattle

⭐ ORIGIN

The Elysian Brewing Company was founded in 1995. In 1996, it opened the door to its 220-seat brewpub on top of Seattle's Capitol Hill. At that time, Seattle was no stranger to craft beer. It seemed that you couldn't turn around in the Emerald City without stumbling over a new brewery or beer. And the entire town was in love with it. Like grunge music, Seattle firmly embraced its small brew scene. When Elysian arrived, there were plenty of other local brews to choose from,

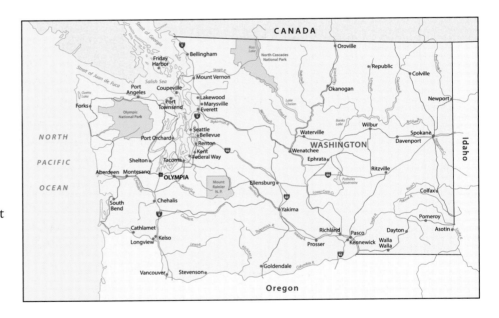

but Elysian, almost overnight, became Seattle's darling.

A year after opening the brewpub, the company opened another location in the very center of town. Right beside the convention center, just a few blocks up from the historic Pike Place Market, and within walking distance of nearly every high-end hotel in the city, an entertainment complex called Gameworks had come to roost. Gameworks is the modern-day equivalent of the neighborhood pizza parlor/video-game arcade. Resembling the loud, flashing, multistory game centers of Tokyo, it sported the latest stand-up arcade games—and featured Seattle's premier brewpub, Elysian.

Today, Elysian has five locations: the original Capitol Hill brewpub; one known as Tangletown in the Greenlake area; Elysian Fields, nestled beside the Seahawks' stadium and the Mariners' ball field; the Elysian Bar; and their production brewery, which isn't open to the public.

WHY THEY ARE AMONG THE BEST

Here is where I confess that I am a fourth-generation Seattleite, and to me, Elysian perfectly epitomizes the Seattle attitude.

Seattle is the kind of place where it rains nearly nine months out of the year, but nobody carries an umbrella. Where people have at least two and probably three outdoor hobbies, and they can go straight from the hiking trail into nearly any restaurant without having to change clothes. Where people care a lot about what music and movies they consume, the type of art they create, and what beer they drink, but less so about what brand of car they drive. Where people are polite, friendly, and easygoing, but at times passive-aggressive and a little uptight. It's the kind of place where nearly anyone can feel at home, and a place where absolutely anyone can find a good meal, a good wine, and a great brew.

Elysian brews beer that you could feel good drinking in the rain. It's the type of beer that goes equally well with hot dogs at the ballpark or with perfectly prepared Copper River salmon or filet mignon. Elysian is a little irreverent, a bit hipster, a little passive-aggressive, and absolutely comfortable being itself. The company's beers are big, bold, smooth, creative, and, above all else, laid-back.

Elysian Brewing offers six year-round beers: The Immortal IPA (6.3% ABV, 54 IBU), Avatar Jasmine IPA (6.3% ABV, 45 IBU), Loser Pale Ale (7.0% ABV, 57 IBU), Mens Room Original Red (5.6% ABV, 33 IBU), Space Dust IPA (7.2% ABV, 62 IBU), and Dragonstooth Stout (7.45% ABV, 60 IBU). It also puts out four regular, rotating seasonals: Split Shot Stout (spring release, 5.6% ABV, 28 IBU), Superfuzz Blood Orange Pale (summer release, 5.4% ABV, 45 IBU), Night Owl Pumpkin Ale (fall release, 5.9% ABV, 18 IBU), and Bifrost (winter release, 7.6% ABV, 58 IBU). The company has a particular love affair with pumpkin beers, releasing several each year. It has organized and sponsored the Elysian Great Pumpkin Beer Festival for ten years running.

AROUND THE STATE

Diamond Knot Craft Brewing, Mukilteo

Diamond Knot Craft Brewing gets its name from a ship that used to transport canned salmon from Alaska down to Port Angeles, Washington. On August 13, 1947, the *Diamond Knot*, full of 154,000 cases of salmon (which at the time amounted to about 10 percent of that year's catch) was hit broadside by another boat, the *Fenn Victory*. The *Diamond Knot* was badly damaged and never made it back to shore. But the rescue and recovery effort that took place in the hours following the collision was nothing short of herculean. Despite a heavy current, barges were brought in, brave divers worked tirelessly, and with the help of a water vacuum, much of the cargo was salvaged. Doesn't that story just make you thirsty? It does me.

My first introduction to their beer was at their original brewery and alehouse, located just steps away from the ferry loading in Mukilteo. The Pacific Northwest is well known for its water (lakes, ocean, and rain), its seafood, and its laid-back atmosphere. A visit to the Seattle area wouldn't be complete without a trip out to one of the islands on a ferry. If you find yourself in a long ferry line in Mukilteo, wander over to Diamond Knot, order a pint of their ESB and a Stonegrill (an entrée of fresh food served with a super-heated stone that you use to cook your own lunch), and enjoy the quintessential northwest experience.

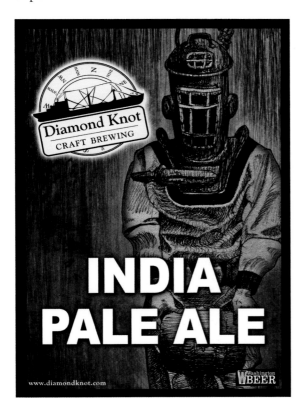

Adam's Northwest Bistro & Brewery, Monroe

Chef Adam is a big, friendly guy with rosy cheeks and a smile that never seems to leave his face. For many years, he was the chef de cuisine at a Seattle institution—Rover's—which sadly closed its doors several years ago. Adam loves food. He loves flavors. He loves making delicious things and sharing them with people. And so, in March 2011, he opened his very own place, which delivers amazing food, paired with fantastic beer. It's a bit of a drive to get out to Monroe, but it's worth the trip.

Washington State

➡ State capital: Olympia

➡ Washington became the forty-second state in the Union on November 11, 1889.

➡ The state is just one of seven in the nation that does not levy a personal income tax.

➡ The Yakima Valley, smack dab in the middle of the state, contains 75 percent of the total hops acreage in the entire United States.

➡ There are 5 million persons of legal drinking age in the state, the average one of whom consumes 24.8 gallons of beer annually.

WASHINGTON, DC

DC Brau Brewing Company, District of Columbia

ORIGIN

DC Brau Brewing Company was founded in 2009 by Jeff Hancock and Brandon Skall, making it the first brewery to operate within the District of Columbia since 1956. In 2011, Jeff and Brandon signed a distribution deal that allowed them to get their locally brewed beer into the hands of the bars, restaurants, and pubs of DC so that the beerly devoted could finally be treated to suds from their hometown.

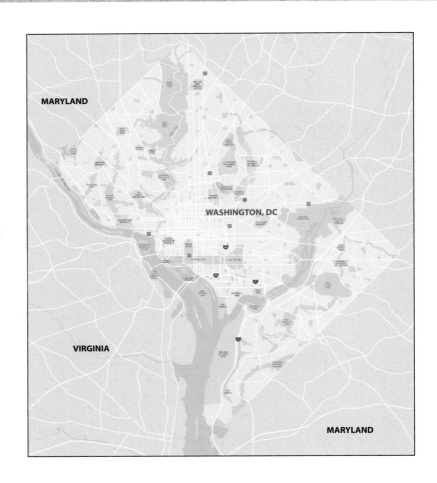

WHY THEY ARE AMONG THE BEST

One thing that sets craft breweries apart from the larger mass-production commercial breweries is their connection to their local communities. Many craft breweries don't distribute outside the borders of their own state or even town. They come face-to-face with their fans on a daily basis, and many take an active role in the community, finding ways to help support or improve the lives of those who drink their beer. The folks at DC Brau are no exception. They donate the spent grain from their brewing process to a local family-run farm to be used as animal feed. Being from DC means that they also have taken an active role in politics. Current law makes it illegal within the city limits for breweries to allow consumption of alcohol on their premises. DC Brau is currently supporting a bill before the DC city council that would allow visitors to actually sample the beers while on-site.

DC Brau's flagship beers include The Public (pale ale, 6.0% ABV), The Corruption (IPA, 6.5% ABV), and The Citizen (Belgian ale, 7.0% ABV). In addition, it has several rotating special releases: On the Wings of Armageddon (imperial IPA, special release, 9.2% ABV), Penn Quarter Porter (5.5% ABV), and Stone of Arbroath (Scotch ale, 8.0 ABV). On a semiregular basis the owners put out draft-only brews that can be found in better bars, pubs, and restaurants across DC. These are a special treat and subject to change based on the whims of the beer muses.

AROUND THE DISTRICT

■ Atlas Brew Works, District of Columbia

Atlas Brew Works was born out of friendship. Two men, Justin Cox and Will Durgin, both engineering students at Vanderbilt University, met and bonded over their love of craft beer. They raised their glasses in toasts, talked of the glorious benefits of beer, and dreamed of one day opening a brewery. When college ended, the two men plunged into their passion. Justin started his beer journey as a home brewer, crafting award-winning recipes using a home-brew kit lovingly gifted to him by his wife. Will headed out to the Master Brewer's program at UC Davis in California to get his professional brewers certificate. The doors opened at Atlas in early 2013. The owners moved into a 9,200-square-foot facility and installed a twenty-barrel brewhouse. Their recent entry into the American craft brewing scene does make them one of the new kids on the block, but new kids often bring fresh, interesting perspectives. Such is the case with these fellows.

WEST VIRGINIA

Mountain State Brewing Company, Thomas

★ ORIGIN

Mountain State Brewing Company is the largest full-scale microbrewery in West Virginia. The brewery was founded by Brian Arnett and Willie Lehmann, both West Virginia natives. Both men started their beer-infused journey when curiosity and the creative urge struck sometime in the early nineties. Digging their parents' home-brew kits out of the attic, they began experimenting and found that they were actually pretty good at making beer. Fast-forward through years of experience and countless home brewed batches of beer, and in October 2005, the two men sold their first beer as Mountain State Brewing.

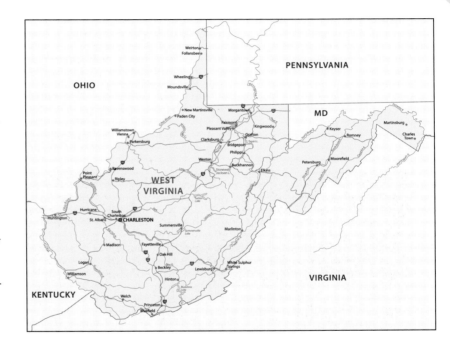

WHY THEY ARE ONE OF THE BEST

You need look no further than the names on their beers to realize that the boys at Mountain State Brewing are deeply connected to their home. Almost Heaven is a reference to John Denver's ode to West Virginia, "Country Roads." Miner's Daughter is a reference to the immigrant coal miners who helped build the state and create its heritage. Seneca Indian Pale Ale is an homage to the Seneca Indians who called West Virginia their home so many years ago. Brian and Willie's beers reflect not only their passion for their home but also the best the state has to offer.

In a way, craft brewers are the unelected representatives of their states. Part of the fun of drinking craft beer is in knowing where your beer comes from, in comparing beers from different places, and in expanding your horizons by taking a journey across the nation through the eyes and hearts of the brewers. Brian and Willie help take us on this journey, showing us around the history and the beauty of the state of West Virginia, one sip at a time.

They brew five beers at Mountain State Brewing Company: Cold Trail Ale (blonde, 5.5% ABV), Seneca Indian Pale Ale (5.4% ABV), Almost Heaven Amber Ale (5.2% ABV), Miner's Daughter Oatmeal Stout (5.3% ABV), and Rumsey Rock Porter (seasonal release, 5.5% ABV).

AROUND THE STATE

Bridge Brew Works, Fayetteville

The fine folks at Bridge Brew Works put out fourteen different beers. Two of those are available year-round: Bridge Brew Ale (draught only, 5.5% ABV, 45+ IBU) and Long Point Lager (draught only, 4.6% ABV). Five are limited releases, meaning they are brewed in small batches several times a year. Those are Baltic Porter (7.0%–7.2% ABV), Belgian-Blonde Trubell (9.2% ABV), Belgian-Style Dubbel (6.5%–7.0% ABV), Belgian-Style Tripel (8.9%–9.2% ABV), and India Pale Ale (7.4% ABV). The rest are seasonally available: Black Lager (available winter and spring, 5.0% ABV), Coffee Stout (available winter, 5.2%–5.5% ABV), Kölsch-Style Beer (available summer, 5.7% ABV), Oatmeal Stout (available fall and winter, 4.2% ABV), Oktoberfest (available September and October, 6.4% ABV), Old Burly Barleywine (available fall and winter, 9.0%–9.2% ABV), and Pale Ale (available summer, 5.8% ABV).

Big Timber Brewing Company, Elkins

Big Timber Brewing Company has a motto: "We make different brews for different crews." They've been at it since 2014, and the future looks bright, bubbly, and full of hops. They feature six staples available year-round: Porter (6.5% ABV, 33 IBU), IPA (6.5% ABV, 70 IBU), Pale Ale (5.2% ABV, 38 IBU), Double Bit IPA (8.0% ABV, 77 IBU), Blonde (4.0% ABV, 17 IBU), and Logger Lager Pils (5.2% ABV, 35 IBU). They also offer six seasonals: Wild & Wonderful West Virginia Wet Hop (5.6% ABV, 40 IBU), Frost Notch (7.6% ABV, 30 IBU), Forestfest Octoberfest (5.6% ABV, 24 IBU), Bourbon Barrel Porter (6.8% ABV, 33 IBU), Sluice Dry Stout (5.2% ABV, 34 IBU), and Hatchet Session IPA (4.2% ABV, 46 IBU).

West Virginia

➡ State capital: Charleston

➡ West Virginia's nickname is the Mountain State. Its motto is "Mountaineers Are Always Free."

➡ The state covers a total area of 24,231 square miles, ranking it as the forty-first largest in size in the Union.

➡ West Virginia was the only state to have achieved sovereignty by proclamation of a US president. It was declared a state on June 20, 1863, by Abraham Lincoln.

➡ There are 1.4 million persons of legal drinking age in the state, the average one of whom consumes 30.3 gallons of beer annually.

WISCONSIN

New Glarus Brewing Company, New Glarus

ORIGIN

New Glarus Brewing Company was founded in 1993 by husband and wife duo Daniel and Deborah Carey. Dan started his career in professional brewing at the age of twenty. He is one of those guys who actually uses his college degree—a bachelor's of food science with an emphasis on malting and brewing science. Pretty handy degree for a brewer. But he didn't stop there. He did an internship in brewing in Germany, attended the Siebel Institute to study brewing technology, and passed the Institute of Brewing and Distilling Diploma Examination and Master Brewer Examination as well. It's hard to imagine that there is a better-educated brewer in America today.

Deborah, on the other hand, is the business brains behind the brewery. She

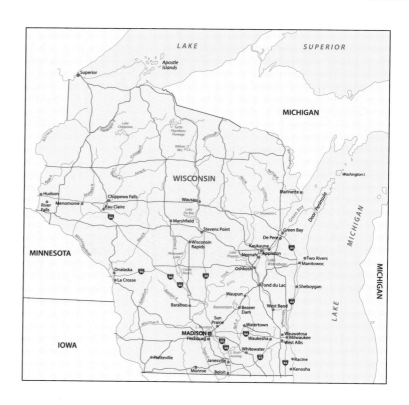

started her first business at the age of sixteen and went on to get degrees in both marketing and business. It was through her hard work, charm, and connections that they managed to raise the startup capital to open New Glarus. Her business acumen through the years has earned her

much deserved recognition and accolades, including an invitation to sit with First Lady Michelle Obama during President Barack Obama's 2013 State of the Union address.

It has been a long journey for the couple. In that first year of production, New Glarus put out just ninety-nine barrels of beer. They grew nearly every single year after that. Twenty years after brewing that first batch, their production was up to 127,000 barrels, and they had made plans for another expansion, which might potentially push their output to double that number of barrels.

WHY THEY ARE AMONG THE BEST

At New Glarus, the Careys pride themselves on using only 100 percent natural ingredients. They draw inspiration from what is fresh right now. Indeed, many of their year-round beers include a fruit component. Over the course of a year, it's quite common to see craft brewers release a seasonal fruit beer, but it's rather unusual to see a brewery with four on their roster year-round. But that's what makes New Glarus so special. It doesn't follow the crowd; it makes its own path. The journey through a raspberry bush can be treacherous, but certainly tasty. And the Careys make it look easy.

New Glarus offers seven year-round brews: Spotted Cow (farmhouse ale, 4.8% ABV), Moon Man (pale ale, 5.0% ABV), Two Women (pilsner, 5.0% ABV), Raspberry Tart (fruit beer, 4.0% ABV), Wisconsin Belgian Red (fruit beer, 4.0% ABV), Serendipity (fruit beer, 4.0% ABV), and Strawberry Rhubarb (fruit beer, 4.0% ABV). They also put out twelve regular seasonals: Fat Squirrel (nut brown ale, available January and February, 5.5% ABV), Snowshoe Ale (amber ale, available January through March, 5.7% ABV), Back 40 (bock, available March through May, 5.5% ABV), Dancing Man Wheat (hefeweizen, available May through August, 7.2% ABV), Staghorn Octoberfest (available August and September, 6.25% ABV), Cabin Fever (pale honey bock, available January through March, 6.0% ABV), Coffee Stout (available February through April, 4.8% ABV), Totally Naked (pale lager, available April through August, 5.0% ABV), Yokel (bottle-conditioned lager, available June through August, 4.2% ABV), Hometown Blonde (available August and September, 4.8% ABV), Pumpkin Pie Lust (pumpkin weisse, 5.5 % ABV), and Black Top (black IPA, 6.9% ABV). From time to time Dan busts loose with a new limited-edition beer. These can be found under the Thumbprint Series label. Expect the unexpected with these beers. There are no guarantees or warrantees issued with these beers, but there are unique adventures available in every bottle.

AROUND THE STATE

▇ Ale Asylum, Madison

Madison's first microbrewery, Ale Asylum offers six year-round beers both in bottles and on tap: Hopalicious (pale ale, 5.7% ABV), Unshadowed (hefeweizen, 6.0% ABV), Bedlam! IPA (7.4% ABV), Ambergeddon (amber ale, 6.7% ABV), Madtown Nutbrown (5.5% ABV), and Demento (4.7% ABV).

The company releases six regular seasonals also in bottles and on tap: Ballistic IPA (available spring to fall, 7.4% ABV), Tripel Nova (available June through August, 9.8% ABV), Kink (Belgian abbey ale, available August through November, 7.4% ABV), Satisfaction Jacksin (double IPA, 9.0% ABV), Mercy (Belgian-style grand cru, available November to January, 10.0% ABV), and Big Slick (stout, October to January-ish, 7.0% ABV). If you are lucky enough to be within striking distance of Madison, drop into the brewpub to try out the brewers' rotating seasonals and their Limited Asylum series, which are recognizable by the orange tap handle.

Central Waters Brewing Company, Amherst

The old brick building that originally housed Central Waters Brewing Company had been many things. Originally it was a Model-A Ford dealership. Years later it became a barbershop. After that it housed a secondhand goods liquidation company. Eventually, in 1988, it was vacated and sat empty until two friends bought it in 1996. After two years of cleaning and remodeling, which included bringing in some used dairy equipment and retrofitting it to make it suitable to brew beer, the Central Waters Brewing Company took up residence, staying in the Junction City building until 2007. The company has gone through several ownership changes, and on the brewery's fifth anniversary the original brew kettle cracked and had to be replaced. Today Central Waters has a new facility in Amherst, Wisconsin. The owners brew eighteen different styles of beer and distribute their delicious beer to more than 200 locations in Central Wisconsin.

Wisconsin

➡ State capital: Madison

➡ Wisconsin has nearly 7,500 rivers and streams. If these were stretched end to end, they would cover 26,767 miles, which is more than enough to encircle Earth at the equator.

➡ On May 29, 1848, Wisconsin became the thirtieth state to enter the Union.

➡ There are 132 active brewing permits in Wisconsin, ranking the state seventh in the nation in total number of breweries.

➡ There are 4.2 million persons of legal drinking age in the state, the average one of whom consumes 36.2 gallons of beer annually.

WYOMING

Snake River Brewing, Jackson

★ ORIGIN

Snake River Brewing is Wyoming's oldest brewery. It has been in operation for more than twenty years, and in that time has amassed a handful of awards from both the Great American Beer Festival (GABF) and the World Beer Cup. In fact, in 2000 and again in 2001, it was named Small Brewery of the Year by GABF. It is currently producing about 8,500 barrels of beer each year, which allows it to distribute to Wyoming, Wisconsin, and New York.

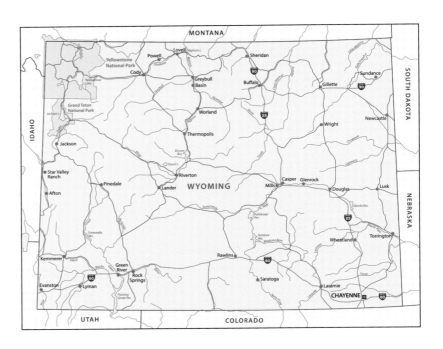

For the first eighteen years of its existence, Snake River packaged its beer in bottles. But like many of the craft brewers in America, it has now switched exclusively to cans. Part of the growing movement into miniature kegs has to do with new canning technology. Not that long ago, putting beer in a can meant that your beer was going to taste metallic. But modern cans are coated to protect the beer, making sure it never comes into contact with the metal, meaning your beer will taste as good—some would say better—out of a can as out of a bottle. Of course, the other reasons for the move to cans are even more powerful. Cans don't let light in, so the beer doesn't degrade from contact with sunlight. Cans are lighter than bottles, making them cheaper and easier to ship. Cans get cold faster than bottles. And aluminum cans require far less energy to recycle, and can basically be reused indefinitely.

WHY THEY ARE AMONG THE BEST

Anyone who is an outdoor enthusiast has heard of Jackson Hole. Whether you are a skier, snowboarder, hiker, wildlife photographer, whitewater river rafter, fisherman, or just general outdoor sport–loving person, there is something for you to do, see, or experience here. The brewers at Snake River Brewing do their very best, one barrel at a time, to pair their beers with the world-class activities and scenery surrounding their brewery. The environment around them is their muse, and the beer they brew is an accompaniment for all the joyous things that come from that landscape.

It would be impossible to list all of the beers they brew and have brewed at Snake River. There is a constant ebb and flow of new and creative concoctions coming and going through their taps. They do, however, have six beers that they put in cans. Those are Pako's IPA (6.8% ABV, 60+ IBU),

Snake River Pale Ale (5.2% ABV, 40 IBU), Snake River Lager (4.8% ABV, 20 IBU), Zonker Stout (6.0% ABV, 36 IBU), Snow King Pale Ale (6.0% ABV, 55 IBU), and Monarch Pils (5.0% ABV, 38 IBU). If you find yourself in Jackson, and are in need of a pint, drop by to see what's on tap. Keep your eyes open for their barrel-aged beers, as well as their certified Organic Beer Number 1 (or OB-1 for short).

AROUND THE STATE

Blacktooth Brewing Company, Sheridan

The Blacktooth Brewing Company is tucked away in the town of Sheridan, Wyoming. Situated in a building that was once a car dealership, it opened its doors in late 2010. For being located in such a small town, the folks at Blacktooth brew a very large number of beers, many of which are experimental, most of which are rotating small batches. The beers change rapidly and can be hard to keep track of, but that's most of the fun. They have at least six of these on tap at any one time, and they offer four year-round beers: Wagon Box Wheat (5.4% ABV, 20 IBU), Indian Paintbrush Ale (IPA,

6.2% ABV, 65 IBU), Saddle Bronc Brown (4.8% ABV, 18 IBU), and Bomber Mountain Amber (4.6% ABV, 20 IBU). Again, small batches, constant rotation, and flavors are subject to change, so stop by early and often.

THE
BLACK TOOTH
BREWING COMPANY

Sheridan, Wyoming

GLOSSARY

ABV: Alcohol by volume. It is the measure of the amount of space the alcohol in a beer takes up as a percentage of total volume. It tells you how strong the beer you are about to drink really is. This is the worldwide standard for measuring the alcohol content in beer.

ABW: Alcohol by weight. It is the measure of the weight of alcohol as a percentage of the total weight of the liquid. To convert ABW to ABV, multiply the ABW by 1.25. Conversely, to get the ABW from ABV, multiply the ABV by 0.8.

ALE: Ales are made with "top-fermenting" strains of yeast, which means that the yeast ferments at the top of the fermentation tank. Top-fermenting yeasts work at warmer temperatures than yeasts used to brew lager beer.

ALTBIER: The word *alt* in German translates to English as "old." Altbiers are German-style brown beers that are typically conditioned for longer periods of time, which produces a beer that is quite smooth and well balanced with less fruitiness.

APA: American pale ales are simply variations on the well-known pale ale. American versions differ from their British cousins in that they are often more hoppy and are sometimes described as having a cleaner, more balanced flavor profile.

BALTIC PORTER: A style of porter originally brewed in the late 1700s. They were brewed to be stronger and more rugged in order to survive the journey across the North Sea without spoiling.

BIÈRE DE CHAMPAGNE: A relatively new style in the beer world, this is brewed using a method similar to creating champagne. These beers are usually fermented for a very long time, and often undergo the same process of disgorgement (freezing and removing the yeast and unwanted material from the bottle) that has been employed in the Champagne region of France for hundreds of years.

BIÈRE DE GARDE: Translated from French, this means "beer for keeping." These beers were traditionally brewed in French farmhouses during the winter and spring and kept for drinking in the summer to avoid problems that can occur with yeast and bacteria when the weather is too warm. They are usually pale in color and quite strong. Also frequently called a saison.

BIÈRE DE MARS: Similar to bière de garde, it is a French farmhouse-style beer that is typically consumed in March.

BOCK: Dark, strong German-style lager that is thought to have been originally brewed by the monks as sustenance during their long periods of fasting.

BOTTLE CONDITIONED: The secondary fermentation that occurs when yeast and sugars are added to the beer right before bottling. This process leads to higher alcohol content and consumes the extra oxygen inside the bottle, allowing the beer to age longer without a negative result.

BRETTANOMYCES: A yeast that contributes tartness to a beer during fermentation. In most beers, *Brettanomyces* is considered a bad thing, imparting what some describe as a "barnyard" flavor to the beer. However, some beers, such as lambics and sour ales, use *Brettanomyces* to intentionally add tartness. This flavor is admittedly an acquired taste.

CALIFORNIA COMMON: Also known as steam beers (see *Dampfbier*), these beers are brewed with a lager yeast but fermented at a temperature that is warmer than is typical for creating a lager. The creation of this style is often attributed to the cost of refrigeration and the dire need to have beer, no matter what.

CASK CONDITIONED: Unfiltered, unpasteurized beer that is conditioned inside the cask—including secondary fermentation. Cask ale is also sometimes referred to as real ale and is served from the cask without adding nitrogen or carbon dioxide.

DAMPFBIER: Translated as "steam beer," this style is unique in that it is an all-barley ale that is warm fermented with a weissbier yeast, usually at temperatures above 70°F. This is a very old style of beer, originating from the Bavarian forest near the border of the Czech Republic.

DOPPLEBOCK: Very full-bodied, strong, German-style lager brewed with a double dose of malt. A stronger version of a bock.

HOPS: The dried blossom of the female hop plant. Hops' closest relative is the cannabis plant from which marijuana is derived. Hops impart bitterness and aroma to the beer.

IBU: The measure of the bittering substances in beer. In general, the higher the number, the more bitter a beer; however, some of this bitterness is counteracted by the sweetness from the residual sugars in the beer. So, if you have a thick-bodied, malty beer with high IBU, it might not taste as bitter as a lighter beer with lower IBU. In other words, simply judging a beer by its IBU can be a mistake.

IPA: India pale ale was first brewed in England for export to British troops and colonists in India during the late 1700s. Though there are several different theories as to how this style came into being, the most accepted is that these beers were brewed with more hops and at a higher alcohol content in order to stand up to the long voyage from England to India and arrive in drinkable condition.

LAGER: Lagers are made with "bottom-fermenting" strains of yeast, which means that the yeast ferments at the bottom of the fermentation tank. Lagers are brewed for longer periods of time than ales and at colder temperatures.

LAMBIC: Originally brewed in the Pajottenland region of Belgium, lambics are unusual in that they are fermented using wild yeasts and bacteria. The vats of cooled wort are exposed to the open air, allowing the natural yeasts to get into the sugary liquid, which begins the process of fermentation. The resulting brew is often a little sour and fruity, described by some as similar to cider.

MALT: Processed barley that has been soaked in water and allowed to sprout. This germinated grain is then dried, converting the insoluble starch in barley into soluble sugars that can be extracted via boiling water in order to make wort, which is then turned into beer.

MÄRZEN: Prior to the invention of the refrigerator, it was difficult to brew beer during the summer months, due to high temperatures and the risks of bacterial infection. The brewing season, then, ran from fall into the very beginning of spring. Märzen beers were often brewed in March (Märzen). They were kept in cold storage during the warm weather and were often brewed to reach a higher alcohol content in order for them to keep well.

PALE ALE: Lighter, often pale in color, these ales are characterized by their higher levels of bitterness.

PORTER: Porter gets its name from its supposed popularity among transportation workers of central London in the 1700s. Too busy to stop for an actual meal during the damp, cold months, porters would drop by a pub and knock back a pint of this thick, dark, nutritious beer to give them energy to continue on with the rigors of their day.

SAISON: A French farmhouse-style beer. It is typically brewed in the spring or winter, then held to be drunk in the summer, in order to avoid the difficulties of brewing during the warmer weather. This name is sometimes used interchangeably for bière de garde.

SCHWARTZBIER: The German name for black beer. Though these beers are dark in color, they are not necessarily heavy or viscous, like stouts or porters. Many are quite light and often have a well-balanced, refreshing flavor.

STOUT: Dark, thick beers. Stout was traditionally the generic term for the strongest porters. The first incarnations were called stout porters and eventually became a category of their own.

WORT: The liquid extracted from barley or other grains after the mashing process. This liquid is full of dissolved sugars, which, when exposed to yeast, are fermented and become alcohol and carbon dioxide—creating beer.

INDEX